A NORTHERN COMMONWEALTH

A NORTHERN COMMONWEALTH
Scotland and Norway

GORDON DONALDSON

SALTIRE

Text © 1990 Gordon Donaldson

Grateful acknowledgement is given to the National Galleries of Scotland for their permission to reproduce in this book the portrait of *Anne of Denmark* (attributed to Varson) and the *Queen Margaret Panel* by Hugo Van Der Goes, reproduced by kind permission of H.M. the Queen.

Printed and bound in Britain by Billings and Sons Ltd, Worcester. Cover printed by A4 Print, Inverness.

Design by Sarah Fraser, Balnain.

The publisher acknowledges subsidy from the Scottish Arts Council towards the publication of this volume.

Published in 1990
by the Saltire Society,
9 Fountain Close,
High Street,
Edinburgh EH1 1TF

British Library Cataloguing in Publication Data:
Donaldson, Gordon
     A Northern Commonwealth: Scotland and Norway.
     1. Scotland. Foreign relations with Norway, history
     2. Norway. Foreign relations with Scotland, history
     I. Title
     327.4110481

ISBN 0-85411-044-5

CONTENTS

GENEALOGICAL TABLES

FOREWORD

The immediate stimulus to the writing of this book arose from the seventh centenary of the death in September 1290 of the 'Maid of Norway', that 'King's daughter of Norroway' – daughter of a Norwegian king – who was Queen of Scots by descent and who, as she was betrothed to the heir of the English throne, might have been Queen of England also. The commemoration involved the recall of many historic links among these three kingdoms in the course of their varying fortunes over the centuries, and it seemed appropriate to emphasise in particular the manifold associations of Scotland with Norway.

The theme had been in my mind for many years and I have spoken frequently and written occasionally about various aspects of it. In putting material together on the topic I have drawn a great deal not only on historical sources but on what I have learned by experience: I have, during nearly seventy years, travelled through the northern countries and voyaged over the seas which the vikings traversed more than a millennium ago.

In the course of my travels I have often reflected on the existence for some centuries of what can be called a kind of northern commonwealth of nations or North Atlantic Community, stretching from the Baltic to the Greenland settlements, through Sweden, Norway, Denmark, Shetland, Orkney, the Faroes and

Iceland and from the North Cape to the Isle of Man
and Normandy. Essentially one language, one race,
one culture, one set of political and legal institutions,
extended over most of that wide area.

Scotland comes much into the pattern, for Scotland's
northern isles, now peripheral to the British kingdom, were at the very centre of that ancient, sea-
based community. Lerwick, in Shetland, is almost
equidistant from Aberdeen in Scotland, Bergen in
Norway and Thorshavn in Faroe.

Over the centuries the old unity has been disrupted.
The political link was the first to go. There are now
six or seven distinct political units, and Orkney and
Shetland have for five hundred years been attached
politically to a state which was not itself part of that
community. Other aspects of the old association –
language, race and culture – have been eroded. Yet
much survives, in speech, place-names and artefacts,
to recall the past.

Scholars writing on the medieval period often use
the archaic forms of Scandinavian names which they
find in their sources, but I have preferred to use
either the modern equivalent or a form which has
become conventional by literary usage. In Norway
and Faroe, where two forms of a place-name may be

in use, it is difficult to attain consistency and at the same time make the name intelligible to someone who wants to find it on the map. On Norwegian names I have benefited from the help of Mr. Eystein Sedberg. With Shetland names I have rejected some of the monstrosities of the map-makers and have preferred forms reflecting local pronunciation and probable etymology.

I record my gratitude to Mr Imlach Shearer, who kindly read my typescript and made valuable suggestions, and to Major Björn Sedberg, who gave me information about the Norwegian Church in Leith and the Caledonian Society of Norway.

Gordon Donaldson
September 1990.

I SCOTLAND'S NEAREST
CONTINENTAL NEIGHBOUR

The proximity of Scotland to Norway caught the attention of Samuel Johnson when he was on tour in 1773: at Slains Castle he observed that 'from the windows the eye reaches over the sea that separated Scotland from Norway', a remark 'improved' by his companion James Boswell to 'the windows look upon the main ocean and the King of Denmark is Lord Errol's nearest neighbour'.

Norway is indeed Scotland's nearest continental neighbour. From Buchan Ness (10 miles north of Slains) to the nearest point of the Norwegian coast, near Stavanger, is less than 300 miles; from the Berwickshire coast to the Dutch coast, the next shortest distance between Scotland and any point on the continent, is a good deal more.

These simple geographical facts, which did much to shape events for centuries, are often ignored, for no better reason than that Scotland is part of an island which extends southwards until it is separated from the European continent by only twenty miles of sea at the Straits of Dover. Partly because in recent generations there was a preoccupation with travel by land, and partly because Scottish attitudes were influenced by the belief of the English – correct in their own context – that France is the nearest continental neighbour, Scots tend to discern continental links by looking to the south rather than to the east, while the fact that Scotland has shorter routes to the continent than those through England has been obscured. Air travel, which makes land masses irrelevant and southern Britain neither easier nor more difficult to cross than any stretch of sea, should have corrected the emphasis, but the habit of looking to the south is firmly engrained.

This outlook still distorts historical thinking. For example, in the era of the reformation much emphasis is laid on a handful of Scottish intellectuals and divines who sojourned in Geneva and were, so it is claimed, the channel by which Calvinist influence predominated in Scotland. But this land-based, south-looking and almost anglocentric attitude ignores facts which had a far more extensive effect. At that time probably one in every two of the ships sailing from Scottish east coast ports were trading to Lutheran lands, and for every Scot who knew what was going on in Geneva a dozen knew what was going on in the Scandinavian countries.

The means of travel at the disposal of our ancestors shaped a different outlook. Travel by land was slow, uncomfortable and often dangerous until stage by stage – but only stage by stage – the advent of good roads, the steam railway and the internal combustion engine eliminated the disadvantages. Accustomed as we are now to travel in a closed and heated train or car, we overlook the discomfort inseparable from travelling on foot or on horseback in earlier days. One must think of trying to ride in a blizzard of snow over Soutra or Drumochter or through Glen Lochy from Tyndrum to Dalmally.

By contrast, travel by sea offered some advantages. True, the time taken for any voyage under sail was unpredictable, but a ship's motion could be less up-setting than bumping and jolting over rough tracks, and sea-travel was the only form of travel which offered anything like normal comforts. Only on a ship could one have shelter from rain or snow, a fire to warm the body and on which to cook food, and a comfortable bed. In the nineteenth century steam made sea travel more rapid and reliable, and well within living memory there were passengers on ships from Scottish ports to London and from Leith to Aberdeen and Wick.

All through the centuries, people who were habi-tuated to transport by coastal shipping within their own country readily took to the sea for transport to other lands. And, while individuals or small groups might journey to the continent through England, transport by land, except for very short distances, was not practicable for goods. In the middle ages there was often no alternative but to use the sea for transport direct from Scottish ports to any continental country.

On the other side of the North Sea there was a country – Norway – where, because of high and steep mountains, land transport was even more difficult than it was in Scotland; a people practised in taking to the waters of their long fjords and the sheltered corri-dor provided by the offshore islets or skerries – the Skjaergård – readily ventured on the open sea.

Voyages between Scotland and Norway presented few serious problems even in the earliest times. On the Scottish side there are natural stepping stones for

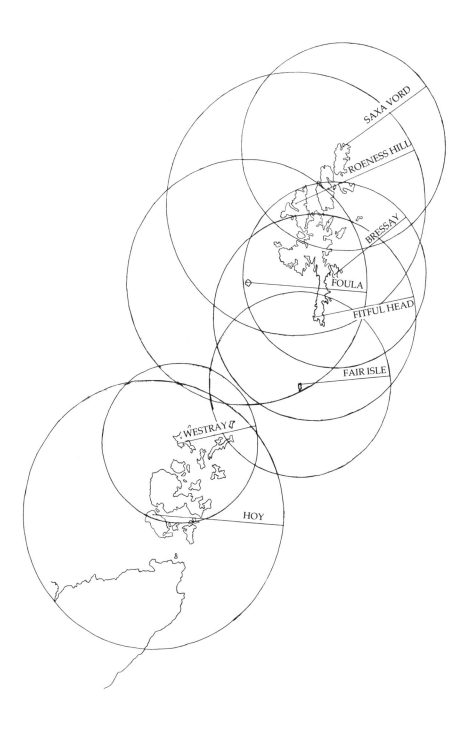

Shetland.

A map showing the area from which the highest peaks in Orkney and Shetland are visible from sea level indicates that there are good chances of picking up Orkney from Scotland and Shetland from Orkney. (Incidentally, that map shows what the men on Agricola's fleet were looking at when they rounded the north of the Orkneys and 'Thule was seen in the distance' – no doubt Fair Isle and Fitful Head but, far more impressive, the more remote mass of Foula looming through a haze. This raises the speculation whether 'Foula' indeed derives from the Norse for 'bird island' or if it may perhaps be related linguistically to 'Thule' – a speculation perhaps no more fanciful than the supposed association of Charybdis and Corrievreckan.)

Beyond Shetland, the stretch of open sea to Norway was a far more considerable obstacle than any crossing between Scotland and Shetland, for a vessel lost sight of one coast long before it reached the other, even under the most favourable conditions. But it was not formidable to navigators with any experience. The Norwegian coast, on its side, is very long, running almost due north and south where it is in the same latitudes as Shetland, Orkney and the north of Scotland.

On the other side, Shetland is likewise long from north to south, and account must again be taken of the areas of sea from which the heights in Orkney and Shetland can be seen. The voyager from Norway was approaching a large area where, with good visibility, there was every chance of picking up land.

There has been much speculation about the navigation of early mariners, without such instruments as compass, log, chronometer and some equivalent of a sextant. There were various devices by which they could be sure of holding their latitude and so keeping a vessel on a course east or west, but those observant men knew fairly accurately how far the sun was above the horizon at any time of the day and year in the lands from which they had set out, and they made it their business to keep on a course which showed the same elevations of the sun.

Besides the sun, these men knew the stars. The elevation of the Pole Star, in particular, could be taken, perhaps more easily than that of the sun; but apart from that, sailing at night and keeping the Pole Star on the beam, they would know if they were holding their latitude. Apart altogether from the element of calculation and from the whole matter of holding a course, they could make deductions from the flight of birds and even from the appearance of the surface of the sea, to arrive at an estimate of the distance and direction of the nearest land. It must be remembered, too, that massed clouds, following the configuration of the land beneath them, can give a clue to the presence of land which is itself below the horizon. A modern navigator, with the latest instruments, can read off from dials in the wheelhouse his latitude and longitude and know his position without raising his eyes to the horizon: his medieval predecessor kept his eyes ranging over sea and sky all the time.

It was not insurmountably difficult, then, for men of the Dark Ages to make the crossing between those two coasts of Norway and Shetland, especially as there are no hazardous tidal currents comparable to those between Shetland and Orkney and between Orkney and Caithness: it is quite unlike the voyage north from Scotland, involving the Pentland Firth and Sumburgh Roost. In some ways the Shetland-Norway crossing is the easier of the two. It does seem that most of the Scandinavian voyagers to Scotland held their latitude across to Shetland and then worked their way south by the 'stepping stones' already mentioned.

It is, as it happens, near its north-eastern extremity that Shetland is closest to Norway. While Bergen-Lerwick measures 187 nautical miles (as compared with 183 from Lerwick to Aberdeen), the shortest crossing between Shetland and Norway is more than 20 miles less. From Balta Isle, off the east coast of Unst, it is only 161 miles to Utvaer light, on the most westerly islet off the Norwegian coast, lying well out from the mouth of Sognefjord, 50 miles north of Bergen. Of course proximity is not the whole story, because we must again take into account the height of the land and the distance from which the land can be seen at sea. But the map of the visibility of the hills shows that the north end of Shetland is slightly advantageous from this point of view as well. Just to the north-west of Balta Isle, where Shetland comes nearest to Norway, there is the great height of Saxavord, rising to over 900 feet (and so matching Fitful Head and its 900 feet at the south end of the Shetland Mainland). It is no accident that the first landings of the Norsemen in Shetland are traditionally associated with the north-eastern shores of the archipelago.

There is, or was, a tradition in Fetlar, told by a reliable repository of traditions, that the first landing of

Norsemen in Shetland was at Funyie, on the east coast of Fetlar, which would be little farther from Norway than Balta is. Then, the account went on, as they found the Wick of Funyie – rock-strewn and exposed in the south-east – useless as an anchorage or a base, the pioneers went round to the Wick of Gruting. This they must have found unsatisfactory too, for, while it is sheltered from the south and south-east, north and even north-west winds send in heavy seas.

The fact is that Fetlar, with all its conspicuous advantages in fertility, has always been handicapped by its lack of a natural harbour: only elaborate works at Oddsta, near the north-west point of the island, created the modest facilities necessary for the modern vehicle-ferry. The likelihood is that any early settlers who had landed in Fetlar would soon move on to Unst, where land-locked Baltasound offered all they needed. There is some reason for believing that Norwegian headquarters in Shetland were at first in the centre of Unst, before they moved to Tingwall. Yet visitors who made the land south of Unst or Fetlar would be likely to pick up the Ward of Bressay and the striking Noup of Noss, which would lead them into Bressay Sound, the site of modern Lerwick.

II MIGRATION: FARMERS, RAIDERS AND TRADERS

The story of the Norse impact on Scotland is a longer and larger story than is often thought. As attention is always apt to focus on the picturesque, the romantic and the violent, the features which live in popular memory are raids by marauding 'vikings' and possibly also the great expeditions by Norwegian kings bearing the glamorous names of Harald the Fairhaired and Magnus Barelegs.

But the 'viking raids' extended over no more than some two hundred years before 800 to before 1000 – and royal expeditions occurred on an average rather less frequently than once in a century. In the course of Scoto-Norwegian interaction extending over at least six hundred years there were many other features, not all marked by violence.

Besides, the Norwegian incursion into Scottish history was only a small part of a vast movement of Scandinavian expansion which affected most of western Europe and extended eastwards as well. In England we hear mainly of 'Danes', and although it is true that most of the identifiable invaders of England came from Denmark, such a generalisation (not unknown in Scotland also) is somewhat misleading. The first Scandinavian raiders known to have touched the English coast, in 786 and 802, were said to have come from Hordaland (the hinterland of Bergen) in Norway; in the tenth century there was substantial movement of Norwegians from Ireland (which they had reached by way of the Western Isles) to the north-west of England; and in one of the final phases of the 'Danish' assaults on England, in the 990s, Olaf Trygvasson, a future king of Norway, played a prominent part.

In the period when Scandinavian settlements were well established over vast areas of western Europe commerce was important among their activities, and it has been noted that finds of artefacts, especially coins, are mainly connected with trading centres in the Baltic and Russia and the routes by water both eastwards and westwards, as well as with rich farming districts. Yet it would be difficult to see trade as the main initial incentive for all the far-flung settlements. It seems most likely that the earlier migration westward from Scandinavia was stimulated by nothing more spectacular than the desire to find land from which to raise food.

Norway, especially in the west, was a poor country in terms of fertility, for there was little arable land save along some narrow river valleys, on patches of alluvial soil at the heads of fjords and occasional level shelves on mountain sides. At present only 3.2% of Norway is farmland; 21.7% is 'productive forest'; mountain and moorland make up 61.6%. Thus pressure of population on subsistence might well have led some people to seek new homes overseas in the west as well as to seek chances of plunder. While land-hunger as well as a search for trading opportunities could and did lead to Scandinavian emigration eastwards across the Baltic into Russia (which itself meant movement by sea and by rivers), the most obvious way out from western Norway was west over sea, to Shetland and from Shetland either north to the Faroes, Iceland, Greenland and ultimately America, or southward to Orkney, Caithness, Sutherland, the Western Isles, Man and Ireland. The number of migrants, out of what must have been a meagre and thinly spread Norwegian population, can never have been great, and their achievements are creditable to their courage, stamina, intelligence and enterprise.

Those who are not familiar with the northern lands may jump to the conclusion that to emigrate from the harsh conditions of Norway west to the islands would be a case of 'out of the frying pan into the fire' – an inappropriate metaphor when one reflects on Norway's icefields and glaciers – and that those islands could not support many immigrants. But this is not quite so. Orkney in particular is rich by almost any standards, and quite astonishingly fertile in comparison with other northern lands. Just how remarkable it is can hardly be appreciated except by those who have seen Norway, the Faroes and Iceland and indeed the more barren parts of the north mainland of Scotland.

Offering great opportunities for farming, the kindly Orcadian landscape must have been a tremendous magnet for all the peoples within reach of it as soon as men started to move across the seas at all, and this explains why there are in Orkney, still visible to the eye, ample remains of a whole series of cultures, evidence that all along, these islands have been the home of a prosperous community.

Shetland is a much poorer land than Orkney, but it offers scope for modest agriculture as well as for pasture and it is a land of plenty compared with much of Norway, the Faroes, Iceland, Greenland and parts of north and west Scotland. The Faroes, only marginally north of Shetland, are just on the fringe of cereal cultivation: poor oats can be grown, but the main crop now is potatoes and the main land-based resource in their gaunt landscape is grazing for sheep, as the archipelago's name suggests. Iceland is beyond the area where cereals are practicable, but there are broad valleys and plains where numbers of sheep can graze.

Largs: Scene of Battle, 1263.

South-western Greenland, where colonists from Norway settled, lies in the same latitude as Bergen and is three or four degrees south of the southern shores of Iceland. The coast is largely fjord country like western Norway, providing much sheltered water, and in favourable weather presenting a quite mellow appearance at variance with its reputation for 'icy mountains'; it offers pasture, but the extreme poverty of most of its soil, as well as the remoteness

Lumbister: Western Approach to Portage.

of the place, made it the one insular Norse colony which failed. Some of the Scottish western highlands and islands are as poor and barren as Norway, and most of Lewis and eastern Harris cannot have had much appeal, but islands like Colonsay, Gigha and Isla have great potential fertility.

The whole prospects west over sea from Norway were not unattractive to land-hungry migrants, seeking above all else ability to produce food. And all those lands, in addition to their possibilities for agriculture and the keeping of flocks and herds, offered elements of life familiar in the Norwegian homeland – fishing in the surrounding waters, and the fowling-cliffs with their produce in birds and eggs.

The motives for the movement from Norway west over sea are obvious, and, while it is impossible to ascertain when it began, it can be guessed that it began long before the dates for which there is evidence. Apart from the comparative ease of making a landfall, there is a meteorological point to be kept in mind. It is always possible to rely on a spell of easterly winds in the spring or early summer, while at other seasons westerly and south-westerly winds prevail. Thus, as soon as men in Norway learned that there was land to the west, they knew they could count on reaching it with the easterly winds at the beginning of the cruising season and that they could equally depend on westerlies to bring them back in the course of the summer or at the end of the summer.

That men in Norway first learned that there was land to the west through the chance arrival on their shores perhaps of wooden artefacts or perhaps of storm-driven and involuntary voyagers is a reasonable conjecture. Examples of such voyagers have been authenticated. The most widely publicised was Betty Mouat in 1886. A woman of sixty, she set out on 30 January 1886 from her home at Scatnes, near the southern tip of the Shetland Mainland, to proceed to Lerwick, 25 miles to the north, on the smack *Columbine*, with a skipper, mate and seaman. About half an hour out, a sudden swing of the boom swept the skipper and mate overboard and, although the mate managed to haul himself back on board, the skipper was rapidly left astern. The two men on board launched the small boat, but failed to find the skipper. Meantime the *Columbine*, her sails filled, drove on at such speed that to overtake her was impossible. Efforts were made by other vessels to find the fugitive but she was not sighted. Alone, with little food and battered by the elements, Betty Mouat had a miserable time, but after eight days and nights at sea the smack, escaping many hazards as she approached a rock-bound coast, almost miraculously drifted ashore on the island of Lepsöy, nine miles north of Ålesund.

There was a tradition in Ulsteinvik, not far north of the island of Selje (which figures in another tradition of castaways), that a woman had drifted there from Shetland in 1815 and married the man who rescued her when she stranded on her arrival in Norway.

Something more than tradition vouches for what is related of castaways from Shetland in 1745. Two girls who were in service with the laird of the island of Uyea, off the south of Unst, went to the island of Haaf Grunay, a mile to the east, to milk cows which were pastured there, but after collecting the milk a westerly wind prevented them from returning to Uyea and drove them out to sea. Like Betty Mouat they took eight days to reach Norway, but unlike her they married there and settled in the island of Karmöy, south of Haugesund on the south-west coast.

There are other, less substantiated, traditions, in different parts of Norway, of girls arriving there from various lands overseas. One wonders whether they perhaps owe something to the legend of St. Sunniva. She was the Christian daughter of an Irish king, and to escape the importunity of a pagan viking chief who wanted to marry her she fled with a group of men, women and children who seem to be thought of as a Christian community shunning an evil world. Embarking on three ships, they rejected any means of shaping their course but committed themselves to the elements, and were carried across the ocean to the island of Selje, between Ålesund and Bergen. The country was still predominantly pagan and under the rule of the strongly anti-Christian Haakon Jarl (c. 970-90). Thus threatened afresh, the company took refuge in a cave and prayed for death, whereupon a landslide sealed up the cave and they all perished. Later on, some merchants sailing past the island saw a mysterious light and, going ashore, found a human hand which emitted a fragrant odour. This was reported to Olaf Trygvasson, the first Christian king of Norway, who commanded a search, which revealed the body of Sunniva, perfectly preserved.

A church, and later a monastery, were established on the island, which became for a time the seat of a bishopric. But in the eleventh century the bishopric of Bergen was established and the relics of Sunniva were moved to the cathedral there (1170). Payments were made from Shetland towards the upkeep of Sunniva's shrine at Bergen and there was a chapel dedicated to her on the island of Balta, off Unst. The saint's name was not infrequently given to girls in Shetland in the sixteenth and seventeenth centuries and has recently been revived, partly because it was used for three successive ships, the first of which pioneered regular cruises from Leith to Norway and all three of which linked Shetland to Scottish ports.

While Shetland may very well have been the first land to be reached by sporadic adventurers overseas from western Norway, it is not the first landfall for which we have historical proof. There is a good deal of information to suggest that something like a major irruption of Scandinavians began about the end of the eighth century. The Anglo-Saxon Chronicle places the beginning of what the people of England saw as 'the northern terror' in 786, and in 794 and 795 there were raids on Ireland and on Iona, which was re-visited in 802 and 806. The Emperor Charlemagne foresaw the perils to his dominions from this north-ern menace before he died in 814, and all western Europe seemed vulnerable. The first known raid by Danes in the south of England was on Sheppey at the mouth of the Thames in 835, by mid-century they were wintering in the south-east of the country and about the same time there was an isolated attack on Northumbria. All probability suggests that Scandina-vians had reached the Scottish islands at much earlier dates and one can even speculate whether the 'sea pirates' who in 618 burned to death St. Donnan 'with a hundred and fifty martyrs' in Eigg represented forerunners of 'the vikings'.

III THE 'VIKING' SHIPS AND THEIR SCOTTISH DESCENDANTS

Much of the spectacular success of the Norsemen in exploring, raiding and colonising was due to the superlative qualities of their ships. It would appear that over a thousand years ago some unknown genius in the north devised a method of boat construction and a shape of hull with qualities which have never been improved on since and which produced the most seaworthy open boats ever made. Boats built from slender planks on ribs probably developed from boats constructed of skins stretched on frames consisting of branches.

The earliest specimens were flat- or round-bottomed, without keels, and were rowed or more probably paddled, but by the seventh century, as the Kvalsund ship shows, the keel was beginning to develop, and this facilitated the use of a sail and made it practicable to sail close to the wind. Several examples have been found. The best-known collection is in the Ship Museum outside Oslo, where there are vessels discovered in burial mounds several miles down the west side of Oslofjord and carefully reconstructed.

There have been other similar discoveries in both Norway and Denmark, all helping to put together the story of those remarkable craft. One of the more recent and most remarkable finds was made in Roskilde Fjord in Denmark, where some vessels had been filled with stones and sunk as blockships about the year 1100. When they were discovered in 1957 they were in such a fragmented condition that a film showing the process of reconstruction was titled 'The jigsaw of a million pieces'. It turned out that there were three merchant ships, of a type which would perhaps be used in conveying settlers and their goods, of varying sizes down from about 70 feet long, a single warship 60 feet long and a vessel apparently intended for conveying passengers in sheltered waters.

Among the exhibits at Oslo is what is probably the best known of all 'viking ships', the Gokstad ship, discovered in 1880 and dating from about 850-900, 76 feet long and 17 feet of beam, with 32 oars. The longship *par excellence,* built for ocean-going, it has superb lines. Its light hull, built of planks or strakes first riveted together and then lashed to the ribs or frame with spruce-roots, gave such flexibility that the gunwale could twist up to six inches without loss of stability. The whole construction is of oak, and the keel, which provided basic strength, was made of a single piece of oak, from a tree with a trunk about 80 feet high. A replica, built in 1896, crossed the Atlantic in four weeks, reaching speeds of 10-11 knots. No Norwegian oak could then supply the keel in one piece, and suitable timber had to come from Canada.

The Gokstad ship's neighbour in the display, the Oseberg ship, discovered in 1904, is slightly shorter, at 72 feet, and slightly broader, at 18 feet with only 30 oars. Also of oak, it is of the same general pattern, but is far more ornate and looks as if it had something

of the character of a state barge rather than a sea-
going vessel or a fighting ship. Associated artefacts
include tubs, a decorated cart, a sleigh, a tripod, three
beds and textile material. It is believed to have been
used in the burial of a queen.

Alongside these great showpieces in the Oslo
Museum is a much smaller boat with the same general characteristics, suitably modified for its size, and
this is in some ways more suggestive, for it resembles
the small boats for everyday use which are still to be
seen around the shores of all the northern lands and
which demonstrate the merits of their ancient forerunners.

These vessels have three particular qualities which
throw light on the operations of the Scandinavian
adventurers. Firstly, the lines of the hull, curving

New Norwegian boats of traditional design, Bergen 1990.

outwards as well as upwards in both stems and sides, mean that as the boat meets a sea a constantly larger surface is presented to the water, with consequent greater capacity for riding the waves rather than cutting through them.

Such boats may be lively, but their very liveliness makes them buoyant and safe. The shape of the hull has the further advantage that not much water comes inboard when waves break against the sides, whereas waves striking a relatively perpendicular hull break and come inboard. The curved stern, too, unlike a square stern, does not invite a following sea to break over it. Moreover, the frame of the vessel, with relatively few ribs, is flexible and resilient rather than rigid. All those characteristics of seaworthiness were very serviceable in the steep narrow waves of the North Sea and tumultuous tidal streams among the islands.

Secondly, because the bow is curved and not perpendicular, the boat is admirably adapted for running up on a beach. The straight-stemmed boat is apt to strike the bottom before anyone can step ashore dryshod, whereas the overhang from a curved stem makes it easier to so so, and it can be made still easier if some weight is moved aft and force exerted with the oars, so that the boat carries some distance up through the shallows. Then it is possible to set the foot on the bow and step ashore dry.

It is not to be thought that the vikings were afraid of getting their feet wet, but if a man could jump ashore dry instead of with waterlogged clothing he would be in better shape for facing any enemies who might be awaiting him.

A third advantage is that, owing to the curved

stem, the keel is shorter than the over-all length, perhaps only two-thirds of the overall length in a small boat, though the proportions diminish greatly in larger vessels. This means that if a boat is being moved on dry land the surface of resistance is less than is the case in a boat with straight stems. The shortening of the surface of resistance might not mean very much if only two simple smooth surfaces were in question, but with a boat and a beach there is one smooth surface and one rough surface – sand, shingle, boulders or even rock. To be able to draw a boat up clear of the water with relative ease is always an advantage if there is not a sheltered anchorage.

The short keel had the additional advantage that it made it easier to draw a boat over an isthmus between two stretches of water. Such portages were a conspicuous feature of Norse operations and were all

The Gokstad Ship, probably ninth century.

in the day's work for men from Norway, who were accustomed to country in which there were many isthmuses which provided shortcuts from sea to sea and across which boats could be drawn. The configuration was similar in the West Highlands and Islands of Scotland, where the frequent occurrence of the place-name Tarbert or Tarbet (from two Irish words which together mean 'portage') commemorates what was surely a regular expedient.

There are significant examples in Shetland too. At a point on the Mainland of Shetland, the Mavis Grinnd ('the gate of the narrow isthmus'), only a few yards separate the Atlantic from the North Sea, and drawing a boat across at that point cuts out a great mileage of exposed water. The present writer has taken a boat across from sea to sea at the Mavis

Shetland sixareen, nineteenth century.

Grinnd and also at another Shetland isthmus at the head of Burra Voe in Yell. There are three more places in Shetland where, it seems, boats were habitually drawn across – and these involved 'portages' not of a few yards but of a couple of miles. One of them is from the head of Sullom Voe to Brae. It may be asked, why take a boat across two miles of land there, when the isthmus at the Mavis Grinnd is only a few yards? But the west side of the Mavis Grinnd leads into a tricky bit of water, a kind of funnel into which westerly winds pack the sea and which leads directly into the open Atlantic, whereas the crossing to Brae offers sheltered waters on both sides.

A second place of portage is at Quarff, in the south Mainland, where a striking cleft or gap occurs in the hills. The third of those Shetland places of portage is in North Yell, between Lumbister and Colvister. When Lumbister was inhabited (as it was until the second half of last century), the men kept their boats in summer on the west coast, where they had immediate access to the mouth of Whaalfjord and the open ocean; but in winter they moved their boats across to Colvister, on the sheltered waters of Basta Voe. The first stretch at the west end must have been awkward, where a burn runs through a deep and narrow gorge, but that leads on to a long stretch with not only level ground but two lochs which greatly shortened the actual portage.

Despite all advantages, it was obviously a considerable operation to take boats over such stretches of country, and the comparative ease of moving a small boat, which could be drawn almost anywhere by her

The Mavis Grind, Shetland: Atlantic on right, North Sea on left.

crew of two or four men if she was lightened by the removal of everything moveable – oars, thwarts, floorboards, mast – must be measured against the difficulties which arise with larger vessels. Ease or difficulty in drawing a boat up a beach or over a stretch of land is related to the surface of the ground. Sand is worst, for the keel sinks in, shingle is not much better, and large boulders are awkward. The easiest beach is one with small stones. The task is always eased by using skids, or 'linns' as they are called in Shetland. Pieces of wood are generally used now, but the traditional linns were whale-ribs, which take on such a high polish that the boat simply glides over them.

So far so good. But as the boat becomes larger the task becomes more difficult. It is not only the weight and the bulk that cause complications, but the height of the gunwale. Part of the knack of drawing up a small boat is to put the knee against the overhanging side and lift as well as pull, but it is impossible to do this with a large vessel.*

---

* I had the curiosity to enquire what happened in the case of the sixareens – those massive six-oared boats, up to about 30 feet overall, which were used in Shetland for deep-sea fishing in the nineteenth century – and what the crew of such a vessel could do with her on dry land. I spoke to an old man whose father had been at sea in a sixareen in the disastrous gale of 1881, when so many boats were lost. He told me that his father's boat had managed to make the entrance to Whaalfjord, on the west side of Yell, and they went on up to the head of that five-mile-long inlet. There they were able to draw her up, not entirely out of the water, but with about two thirds of her keel out, so that she was safe.

Now, those sixareens were beamy, heavily-built craft, designed to carry a great bulk of fish; probably a more lightly-built six-oared boat could have been fairly easily managed up a beach by her crew, but it is difficult to see that they could make a long portage. Of course when more than one boat was involved, either when coming ashore or in an operation like a portage at Lumbister, then it was easy to muster two or more boats' crews to manhandle each boat in turn.

It seems very likely that the crew of a viking longship could get her part of the way out of the water and on to a beach, and two or three crews together could get her completely clear of the water. But whether they could take her far over land is another matter. The Gokstad ship is 6′ 4″ from keel to gunwale, which made any lifting motion impossible, though it has been suggested that the oars might have been inserted in the oar-holes and borne on men's shoulders to take some of the weight. As for drawing or pulling power, a harness could have been rigged round the boat and a hawser carried ahead from it so that a team of men could pull: that has been a recognised method of drawing a heavy boat on a beach. Besides, with such a harness rigged, it would be possible to introduce horses or oxen.

One begins to envisage a somewhat elaborate operation: a gang of men either pulling the hawser or goading on the oxen who were pulling; another gang along the sides of the boat to keep her on an even keel; and one or two others withdrawing skids as she cleared each one and laying them down again ahead of her so that she could mount them. It seems on the whole improbable that a great ocean-going longship could have been manhandled over a portage of any significant distance and that such operations were carried out by somewhat smaller vessels. However, the fact remains that operations of this nature were carried out and they must have added enormously to the mobility of the Norsemen on their various expeditions.

IV ROYAL CRUISES AND LANDWARD ASSAULTS

The great majority of the countless expeditions made west over sea from Norway during five centuries and more are unrecorded: many migrants must have voyaged successfully to settle in the islands where their traces can still be found, but we know nothing of the voyages which came to grief in storms or fogs.

Expeditions must have ranged in size from a family or a group of neighbours, through organised raiding parties and bands of colonists under the leadership of their local headman, to the major operations of a succession of Norwegian kings – Harald the Fairhaired in the late ninth century, Olaf Trygvasson at the end of the tenth, Magnus Barelegs a hundred years later and finally Haakon Haakonsson in 1263. Harald the Fairhaired possibly, and Magnus Barelegs certainly, crossed the seas twice.

A fifth Norwegian king, Harald Hardrada, also made an appearance in the northern isles, but merely in passing on his way to do battle with Harold, King of England, in 1066.

It is only on such major expeditions, under royal leadership, that we have any information, but it includes a lot of circumstantial detail.

The story starts from the creation of the Norwegian kingdom. Norway, far-flung and containing relatively small pockets of habitable land divided from one another by almost impenetrable wastes of lofty mountains – though linked together by the waterways around the coast – contained in earlier times a number of petty kingdoms. The most important of them seems to have been in eastern Norway, in the kindly land around Oslofjord, and the massive burial mounds of early kings can be seen on the west side of that fjord, at Borre, near Horten, about 50 miles south of Oslo. It was in similar mounds, a little farther south, that the Gokstad and Oseberg ships were found. That was the area where the kings originated who were to make Norway a single kingdom.

The story of Harald the Fairhaired (or Finehair) is perhaps too romantic to be altogether true. The picturesque details were not written as we know them until about three hundred years after his day, when the Sagas of the Kings were composed by the Icelander Snorre Sturlason, to whom the Norwegians – enlightened people who delight to honour historians – have erected a monument outside Our Lady Kirk in Bergen. But while the details of the narrative have been much criticised, they reflect underlying truths.

The tale is that Harald loved a lady who despised such a petty ruler and declared that she would not marry him until he became king of all Norway. Harald resolved to conquer the whole land and vowed never to cut or comb his hair until he had done so. Needless to say, he was successful, and won the lady's hand. His final victory was at Hafrsfjord, very near Stavanger, supposed to have been fought in 872. It is agreeable to find a date amid so much that is remote and shadowy, but some would put the battle twenty or thirty years later.

Monument in Bergen of Snorre Sturlason, compiler of the Sagas of the Norse Kings.

However, Harald found that some of the leading men whom he had defeated and ousted had fled overseas to take refuge in the islands, and probably they joined forces with vikings who had already made their way there from Norway. To complete and consolidate his supremacy in Norway, Harald had to undertake an expedition, or perhaps more than one expedition, overseas. So, the story goes on, he crossed to Shetland, as the nearest lair of his enemies.

According to a tradition which is surely baseless, he landed first at Haraldswick in Unst. A landing there would be likely enough on geographical grounds, for Haraldswick is only a couple of miles from the point in Shetland closest to Norway, but the mere existence of the name Harald is not enough to justify the story. Indeed the existence there of a mound called (since when one wonders) 'Harald's Grave', tells against the story, for it is not the grave of the Fairhaired King. Besides, if Harald or anyone else landed at Haraldswick, open to the south-east, he would soon have abandoned it for the incomparable harbour of Baltasound two miles to the south. In Shetland, we are told, Harald 'cleared out' the vikings and then moved on to Orkney, where he did the same thing.

He next proceeded to the Hebrides and Man to assert himself there. To perpetuate Norwegian control of the northern isles Harald offered them to Rognvald, Earl of Möre (a district west of Trondheim), who deserved a reward because one of his sons had been killed on the expedition. Besides, Rognvald had undertaken what had surely been a disagreeable task in cutting the king's hair, uncombed for ten years while he was conquering Norway and winning his bride. Rognvald declined the islands for himself and passed them on to his brother Sigurd, with whose descendants they remained for centuries.

In Orkney and Shetland, as in Faroe and Iceland, the Norse settlers did not have the powerful competition from other cultures which they had in Ireland, England and Normandy, and they were able to transplant their institutions to what was almost virgin soil. The earldom of Orkney, founded as a Norwegian dependency by Harald the Fairhaired and for a long time including Shetland, Caithness, Sutherland ('the southern land'), as well occasionally as other territories, had a continuous existence for almost four centuries, though with shrinking boundaries and gradual erosion of some of its Norse character. Not until 1472 was it annexed to the Scottish crown. Another Norwegian dependency was established in the Hebrides ('the Sudreys' or southern isles as seen by Norwegian eyes) and took shape as a principality with its headquarters in Man and known as the kingdom of Man or of Sodor and Man. It ended in 1266, when sovereignty over that area was ceded by Norway to Scotland, but something like its shadow, reviving in the fourteenth century as a lordship of the Isles under native auspices, lingered on until it was annexed to the Scottish crown in 1494. The bishop's see of Man is still styled 'Sodor and Man'.

Harald, it will be observed, had not come as a conqueror of an indigenous population (about whose very existence his saga is silent) but to deal with 'the vikings', who were Norwegians like himself. Those 'vikings', however, had been having their own way with some of the indigenous peoples for a century and perhaps more before Harald came on the scene. Nor was it only by way of the earldom of Orkney and the kingdom of the Isles that Scandinavians were making an impact on Scotland in Harald's days. There is evidence from the Scottish side about battles between Scottish monarchs and Norse invaders not on the fringes of the land but in its centre. A heavy defeat inflicted on the Picts, in eastern Scotland, by 'Danish pirates' in 839, may have helped to drive them into union with the Irish or 'Scots' of the west to form one kingdom ('Alba', the land north of the Forth and Clyde).

As Iona had become untenable for the Scots owing to repeated Norse attacks, relics of Columba were transferred to Dunkeld, which was central in Alba and about as far from the sea as possible, yet even Dunkeld was not safe from versatile enemies who could use rivers as well as the sea. The Clyde estuary and river likewise served the Norse kings of Dublin for entry to the heart of Scotland. It has been suggested that the Norse in Ireland found access to Northumbria not only through Cumbria but by way of the Clyde and the Forth, a route which brought them into collision with the kings of Alba.

Certainly in 877 King Constantine II was defeated by 'Norwegians' at Dollar, just north of the Forth, and then killed in battle at Forgan in north Fife. His successors continued to be under some pressure from Scandinavians who were established not only in the west and north but also in a band of territory stretching across Britain from the Solway to the North Sea.

What happened in southern England, leading in 886

to a partitioning of the country between Alfred and the Danes and the creation of 'the Danelaw' and to the assumption more than a century later of the English crown by a Danish king, has only indirect relevance to Scotland though it is not to be forgotten.

However, the Scandinavian impact on the north of England for a time created for the kings of Alba on their southern frontier not an English kingdom but a Scandinavian one. A 'great army', evidently a composite force, which in 865 landed in East Anglia, was next year in York and soon afterwards in Northumbria. At this stage (870) the Norse king of Dublin, Olaf the White, joined forces with a Norse ruler of York to besiege and capture Dumbarton, the capital of the kingdom of Strathclyde, which extended at least as far south as the Solway. Northumbria was never effectively within the English 'Danelaw', but Scandinavian influence reached it through invasions from Ireland and the Solway area early in the tenth century.

The Alban kings and Northumbria allied against this threat but were defeated in 918 and a Scandinavian kingdom of York was founded. The English under King Athelstan attacked York in 928 and his growing pressure led to an alliance of Olaf, the Norse king of Dublin (whose father had ruled in Northumbria) and other Irish rulers with the kings of Alba and Strathclyde, but this coalition was defeated at Brunanburgh in 937. Olaf came back in 939 to occupy York, he invaded Northumbria in 940 and crossed the Tweed to attack Tyninghame. Erik Bloodaxe, a son of Harald the Fairhaired, had been driven from Norway and after a career at sea descended on Northumbria and ruled York for some years, though his position was contested by Olaf. This kingdom ended in 954.

The military operations in the ninth and tenth centuries, with their impact on central Scotland, seem to have left their mark on folk memory there in a way that the maritime activities of the Scandinavians in the north never did. But probably there was a blur between the doings of Danes from England in the tenth century and those of Norwegians and Orcadians from the north, of which we have evidence in the early eleventh. In the pages of the sixteenth-century romancer Hector Boece they are all 'Danes'. We learn from his pages of the battle of Luncarty, just north of Perth, in 990, which produced a legend about how the Hay family acquired their land in the Carse of Gowrie; and the adoption of the thistle as a national emblem is supposed to date from a Danish attack, planned as a surprise, which was frustrated because one of the invaders, stealthily approaching with bare feet, trod on a thistle.

Boece assigns to the reign of Duncan I (1034-40) some 'weiris aganis the Danis' which ended when 'a new flete of Danis arrivit at Kingorn and the weirmen cum on the land, invading the cuntre with maist cruelte' and the king sent against them 'Makbeith and Banquho', who 'slew ane gret part of Danis and the remanent chasit to thair schippis'. The vanquished paid 'gret soumes of gold' for permission to bury their dead in 'Sanct Colmis Insche' (Inchcolm). Boece cites as evidence for the truth of the story the fact that 'in memory herof mony auld sepulturis are yit in the said insche ingrevin with armys of Danis' – clearly hog-backed tombstones of which one can still indeed be seen in Inchcolm and of which a number survive in some other places, including Govan, which was on the Scandinavians' route inland from the Firth of Clyde, and St. Andrews. Boece concludes that after this defeat it was agreed that 'the Danis sall never cum in Scotland in tyme cuming to move ony weir aganis the Scottis'. One wonders if the ancient rampart known as 'The Danes' Dyke', near Fifeness, may have been associated with those operations in the Firth of Forth area.

Harald the Fairhaired and his contemporaries had been pagans, but not long after his day Christianity began to make some headway in the country, and the Norwegians underwent an official conversion under Olaf Trygvasson, who reigned about 995 to 999. His saga tells us a good deal about his cruises to the west, which seem to have taken place largely before he became king and while he was still a pagan. He spent four years warring and raiding in England, Scotland, the Hebrides, Man, Ireland, Wales and France.

He was associated with a very heavy 'Danish' onslaught on Britain in the early 990s – the period of the alleged battle of Luncarty. At some point in his travels Olaf was converted to Christianity, and his baptism took place in the Scilly Isles. He then spent some time in Ireland and England before heading for home.

Olaf's saga relates that he 'sailed from the west (Ireland) with five ships, first to the Hebrides ... Then he sailed to the Orkneys'. He put into Osmundwall, now known as Kirk Hope, at the south end of the island of Hoy, because the Pentland Firth was not passable. Olaf was not alone in fastening on Kirk Hope as a suitable place to await favourable conditions for crossing the Firth, and he found the haven shared by Earl Sigurd II of Orkney, fifth holder of the earldom, who was on his way to Caithness but had likewise found the Firth impassable.

Olaf was by this time king, and therefore the earl's superior, but it may have been more to the point that he had five ships to the earl's two. At any rate, Sigurd was in no position to disobey a summons to the royal presence. When he appeared, Olaf demanded that 'he must have himself baptized, with all the people of his land, or as an alternative he should die on the spot, immediately; and the king said that he would go through the land with fire and burning, and devastate the land, unless the people were baptized'. The saga goes on with studied understatement: 'and since the earl was thus pressed he chose to take baptism; so he was baptized, and all the people who were there with him'.

Another account has it that Olaf seized Sigurd's three-year-old son at the place where he was being fostered and threatened to kill him in his father's sight unless Sigurd accepted baptism. Yet an other account, which again says that the king threatened the earl's life, adds that Olaf took the earl's son as a hostage. Whatever the detail, the incident recalls a comment on the story that Cardinal Beaton, before his murder, was told, with a sword held at his breast, 'Repent thee of thy former wicked life'; which, it was remarked, 'was a very compendious way of bringing a man to repentance'. After thus compelling Sigurd to accept Christianity at Osmundwall, King Olaf crossed to Norway and made land at Moster, in Sunnhordland, about half way between Bergen and Stavanger.

Sigurd's forcible conversion may well have been somewhat half-hearted. At any rate, in 1014, at the battle of Clontarf in Ireland, he was still fighting under his magic raven banner, which brought victory to the man before whom it was born but death to its bearer, and Sigurd met his end when, after successive standard bearers had been killed, the next candidate for the fatal office thrust the standard into Sigurd's own hands with the words, 'Bear thou thy devil thyself'. However, the long-term consequence of the event at Osmundwall was that Sigurd was Christian enough to be acceptable as a son-in-law to the Scottish king Malcolm II, whose daughter he married and at whose Christian court the son of the marriage, Earl Thorfinn, spent some of his early years.

There was no doubt about Thorfinn's Christianity: during his long tenure of the earldom a bishopric of Orkney was securely established, and for the bishop's seat Thorfinn built a 'minster' or cathedral near his own headquarters at Birsay. Just as the earls of Orkney were subordinates of the king of Norway, so the bishops of Orkney (with those of The Isles, Faroe, Iceland and Greenland) became suffragans of the Norwegian archbishopric of Nidaros (Trondheim) after it was founded in 1152. Thorfinn fitted well enough into the pattern of a triangular relationship of Scotland-Orkney-Norway. It was shortly after his death that Orkney had a visit in passing from Harald Hardrada, king of Norway, on his way to defeat at Stamford Bridge, where two of Thorfinn's sons fought at his side.

Church on Brough of Birsay, Orkney, looking east.

V AN EARLDOM AND THREE KINGDOMS

In the eleventh century the personal and dynastic links between the Orkney earldom and the Scottish kingdom were very close. The details are not always clear, for contemporary Scottish sources, in any event still meagre, show little awareness of what was going on in Orkney, while some saga writers – who, it must constantly be remembered, were not contemporary – had only a sketchy acquaintance with persons and events in Scotland. Amid the confusion, however, certain facts stand out.

The frontier between the earldom of Orkney and the kingdom of Scotland did not then lie on the Pentland Firth. There was a land frontier somewhere on the Scottish mainland, where earldom and kingdom rubbed shoulders. As early as about 980, when rival claimants to the earldom clashed in Caithness, one of them had the support, the Saga says, of the Scottish king and a Scottish earl.

Orkney may have been under some pressure from expansionist Scots, and Earl Sigurd II (c. 980-1014) had for a time to defend Caithness against Scottish attacks. As so often happened, judicious matrimony seems to have been pressed into service to ease tension, and in the very last years of the tenth century Sigurd married a daughter of Malcolm II king of Scots. Their son, Thorfinn the Mighty, apt to be thought of as something like the ultimate viking, was

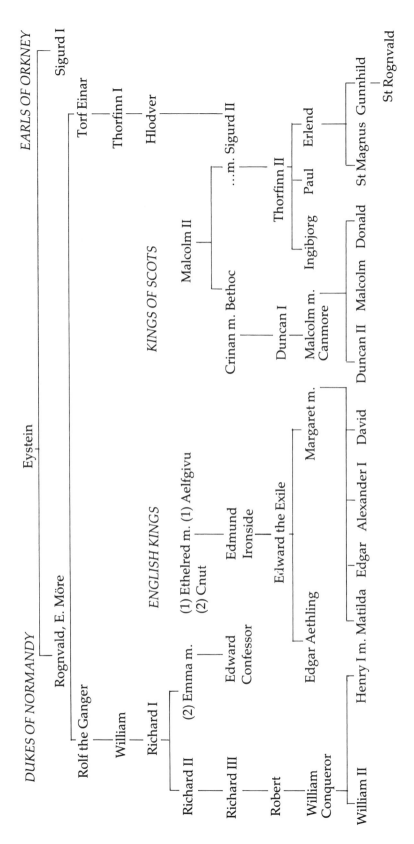

NORMANDY   ENGLAND   SCOTLAND AND ORKNEY

thus half Scots, and to Orcadians he looked like an ugly foreigner, with his black hair, sharp features and swarthy countenance.

The events of Thorfinn's long career as earl (1014-?1065) brought the Orcadian earldom and the Scottish kingdom closer than ever before. When Malcolm II, Thorfinn's grandfather, died in 1034, he left no sons. One of his daughters, Bethoc, had married Crinan, abbot of Dunkeld, and they had a son, Duncan; a second daughter, whose name is not known, was the mother of Thorfinn. It would not have been surprising if Duncan and his cousin Thorfinn had been rivals for the succession to Malcolm.

There was a third claimant, Macbeth, something of a man of mystery around whom fantasies have been woven by writers of fiction among whom William Shakespeare was neither the first nor the last. Dorothy Dunnett based her novel *King Hereafter* on the idea that Macbeth and Thorfinn were one and the same – a startling theory on which the historian W. F. Skene had almost stumbled a century earlier when he observed that 'our authorities for the history of Macbeth know nothing of Earl Thorfinn and his conquests. On the other hand, the sagas equally ignore Macbeth and his doings'.

The view has been put forward that Macbeth's claim to the throne was in right of his wife (who must indeed have had a place in the dynasty, presumably as a grand-daughter of a previous king, for her son Lulach – Macbeth's stepson – was king briefly after Macbeth's death). But even had she been a *daughter* of a previous king that would not have given her husband a right to the throne, any more than Crinan's marriage to Bethoc gave him a right. The most likely source of Macbeth's claim was through his mother, who may have been a daughter of a king, possibly even of Malcolm II. Thus three cousins – Duncan, Thorfinn and Macbeth – may all have considered themselves entitled to the throne when Malcolm II died in 1034. It was Duncan who became king.

It would be understandable if Duncan's two cousins, Thorfinn and Macbeth, then ganged up against him. Duncan certainly had trouble in the north, which might explain what Boece has to say about 'the wars of King Duncan against the Danes'; he was defeated by Thorfinn 'and some say he was slain'. Slain he was, but by the other competitor, Macbeth, and the circumstances strongly suggest that he fell victim to a joint attack by his two cousins, who, after thus disposing of him, partitioned the kingdom between them (1040). Macbeth got the royal title, but Thorfinn, the Saga says, held nine Scottish earldoms, which by any reckoning looks like a generous share, and he is credited with operating as far south as Fife. A continuing alliance betwen the two might explain why they both went on pilgrimage to Rome. True, pilgrimages to Rome were something of a royal fashion at the time: Cnut, the Danish king of England, had gone there, and Edward the Confessor intended to go. Yet Macbeth and Thorfinn, even if they were not one man under two names, may have been fellow-travellers.

After a reign of seventeen years, Macbeth was defeated and killed by Malcolm III (Malcolm Canmore), elder son of the deceased Duncan. The Saga states

that Malcolm took as his first wife Ingibjorg, Thorfinn's widow, but it also states that Thorfinn died
'about the end of Harald Hardrada's days' (and Harald was killed at Stamford Bridge in 1066); if Thorfinn
did not die until in or about 1065, the improbabilities
against such a marriage mount, and it is much more
plausible that Malcolm, eager to ensure the succession after he had overthrown Macbeth in 1057, lost no
time in coming to terms with Macbeth's ally Thorfinn
and marrying Thorfinn's daughter, who may well
have had the same name as her mother. (This matter
is examined in detail in an essay 'The contemporary
scene' in *St.Magnus Cathedral and Orkney's Twelfth
Century Renaissance* [ed. Barbara Crawford, Aberdeen
University Press, 1981].)

However, from the point of view of Scoto-Scandi-
navian relations the precise identity of Malcolm's first
wife matters less than the fact that she belonged to
the ruling house of Orkney and was Scotland's first
Scandinavian queen, which meant that, whatever
other external influences were passed on, southern
influences on Orkney continued to be channelled
through Scotland, and Scandinavian influence on
Scotland continued to be channelled through Orkney.

Already in Thorfinn's day his earldom had a place
in a wider cultural context, for it was now the period
of 'The Normans'. Their 'Northmen' ancestors had
settled in France early in the tenth century under Rolf
the Ganger (so called because his legs were so long
that the native ponies walked out from between them
and he had to walk) *alias* Rollo, first Duke of Normandy, whose cenotaph can be seen in Rouen cathedral.

If Rollo's traditional identification is correct – and, like much else, it has been challenged – he was the nephew of the first Earl of Orkney and the brother of the second. One dynasty ruled two Norwegian colonies: Thorfinn of Orkney, who perhaps just missed being a Conqueror of Scotland, and his contemporary William of Normandy, the Conqueror of England, were distant cousins. To judge from the depictions in the Bayeux Tapestry of the vessels which conveyed William the Conqueror's army across the Channel in 1066, they would have been at home in each other's ships, but in other respects Rollo's descendants had been adaptable and their culture was that of those we call Normans and no longer of Northmen. Yet some writers seem too ready to state or imply that when the barbarous 'vikings' took root in France they were at once miraculously transformed into civilised 'Normans'.

Norman influence began in England long before the conventionally decisive date of 1066. In 1002 the English king Ethelred, familiarly known as 'the Unready', married Emma, daughter of the Duke of Normandy, and she subsequently married Cnut, the Danish king whose dominions included Norway and England. Thus Scandinavian elements, either directly (from Denmark) or indirectly (from Normandy) came together in the ruling house of England. After the death of Cnut, England was ruled briefly by two of his sons, one of them born of a Scandinavian mother and the other the offspring of Norman Emma.

Then in 1042 the English throne went to Edward the Confessor, also a son of Norman Emma, by her first husband, the English Ethelred. The Confessor has been characterised as less an English king than a French monk, and he so surrounded himself with Normans that their ascendancy can be said to have begun with peaceful penetration in his lifetime rather than with armed conquest after his death. Norman William, descendant of Rollo, was not, however, alone in contesting the English throne with Harold Godwinsson after Edward died, for Harald Hardrada, king of Norway, made a bid to renew the Dano-Norwegian ascendancy over England which had existed under Cnut, and Harold of England had to deal with this Northman at Stamford Bridge before being defeated by the Normans at Hastings.

Despite the racial origins of the 'Northmen', by the middle of the eleventh century links between the 'Normans' and the peoples of Scandinavia had become tenuous. Connections, and channels for cultural exchange, existed mainly through Britain, and developments in Scotland were significant. The stages by which southern influence – for a time Anglo-Scandinavian but later Anglo-Norman – reached Scotland can be defined. Duncan I, the first king to rule all of Scotland down to and beyond the Solway, had found his queen in Northumbria. His supplanter Macbeth welcomed Normans who had to flee when there was a temporary reaction against Norman influence in England in the Confessor's reign, and his pilgrimage to Rome suggests that he recognised the importance of continental influence.

Malcolm III ('Canmore' or 'Bighead'), who overthrew Macbeth, was the son of Duncan I and his Northumbrian wife; he spent his formative years in the England of the half-Norman Edward the Confessor during Macbeth's reign, and, with an English estate, this son-in-law of Thorfinn may have been 'a Northamptonshire country gentleman'. It was with southern backing that he was able to prevail against Macbeth; he was 'sworn brother' to Tostig, earl of Northumbria (brother of Harold, the king of England who died at Hastings); he visited Edward the Confessor in 1059 in the company of the archbishop of York and the bishop of Durham. After the termination of his marriage to Orcadian Ingibjorg (whether by her death or by a dissolution on grounds of their relationship as second cousins), he married Margaret, the grandniece of the Confessor and like him descended from Ethelred the Unready, but from Ethelred's first, English, wife and not from his second, Norman Emma.

Margaret was thus more English in race than Edward, but she had spent years in Edward's Normanised court. She had also spent some of her childhood in Hungary. It has been suggested that her enthusiasm for the Christian faith owed something to her experience in Hungary, where Christianity was still an exciting novelty. It is not so often recalled that Margaret's predecessor, Ingibjorg, was a product of the Scandinavian world, where Christianity was almost as much a novelty.

Perhaps Malcolm suffered from two excessively pious wives. He offset the oppressive piety of his household by four times invading the north of England, where the situation after the arrival of the Conqueror in 1066 was singularly unstable, and he brought back so many captives that 'there was not a household in Scotland without an English slave'.

Margaret's brother, Edgar the Atheling, had been

the native candidate for the English throne in 1066, but William the Conqueror had excluded Margaret's kinsfolk from it. When she gave the first four of her sons the names of earlier English kings – Edward, Edmund, Ethelred, Edgar – did she see them as potential pretenders to challenge the Normans? Yet Margaret had herself fallen under the spell of Norman culture and achievement. She corresponded with the Norman archbishop of Canterbury, who sent Benedictine monks to form the core of a community at Dunfermline, a favoured seat of the Scottish king and queen.

In 1093 Malcolm was killed in battle in England, and his dutiful wife expired when she heard the news. The throne was seized, to the exclusion of the sons of Margaret, by Malcolm's brother Donald Bane, who seems to have been brought up during Macbeth's reign not, like Malcolm, in England, but in the western isles; he has been characterised as 'an incorrigible old Celt' but he was as likely to have learned Norse as Celtic ways in the west. Whether Norse or Celtic, he was soon confronted by a Norman element, in the person of Duncan, a son of Malcolm and Ingibjorg, who had been at the court of the Conqueror and his son Rufus for twenty years and now came north with help from Rufus to oust his uncle Donald. Duncan, grandson of Earl Thorfinn, is the first king of Scots of whom we have any depiction: his seal, showing him as a mounted knight, with conical helmet, nose-protector, shield and spear, gives a vivid impression of the Normans riding on to the stage of Scottish history.

The first attempt, by Duncan, at a Norman conquest of Scotland failed, for the wicked uncle, Donald Bane, soon returned and Duncan was killed. Only three years later, however, Edgar, the eldest surviving son of Malcolm and Margaret, arrived, as Duncan had done, with an army supplied by Rufus. An unnamed battle in 1097, when Edgar and his Normans defeated Donald Bane, was the Scottish equivalent of Hastings and an important step towards a Norman conquest of Scotland. Edgar ruled the country as a vassal of the Norman kings of England.

Edgar was the first of an Anglo-Norman dynasty which generation by generation found its queens in England or France and under that dynasty there was an influx to Scotland of Normans who acquired wide lands and filled the highest offices in church and state.

In the general context of the period of the Norman conquest, first of England and then of Scotland, the links of the Scottish royal family with Durham deserve particular mention. Malcolm III, despite his depredations in England, was on amicable terms with the bishop of Durham, in whose company he visited Edward the Confessor in 1059. He must have been familiar with Durham's pre-Norman cathedral, dating from the end of the tenth century with its tower 'of wondrous size'; and shortly before his death he laid one of the foundation stones of the new Norman cathedral. Malcolm's eldest son, the luckless Duncan II, granted to Durham revenues formerly pertaining to the bishop of St. Andrews, and a long series of charters by Scottish kings to Durham runs on through the reigns of Edgar, Alexander I and David. Alexander had a privileged position at Durham, where he was allowed to view the remains of St.

Cuthbert when they were exposed in 1104 on the occasion of their translation to the new cathedral.

Scottish rulers familiar with English buildings and associated with their builders can hardly have failed to imitate those buildings and it does not require great imagination to think of Malcolm Canmore building at St.Andrews a tower of 'wondrous size' like that at Durham or enlarging the old church at Dunfermline along Anglo-Saxon lines; perhaps the captives he brought back from England included masons or even architects. Edgar, Alexander and David were even more familiar with the Norman architec-

St Magnus Cathedral, Kirkwall: nave piers, looking west.

ture of twelfth-century England, and it is beyond credibility that they did not hasten to adopt the new fashion.

The rulers of Orkney had their opportunities to study current architectural fashions both in Scotland and on the continent. No doubt Thorfinn, perhaps already envisaging a 'minster' in Orkney, would keep his eyes open on his way to and from Rome; and – if only when he was campaigning in Fife – he would also see buildings of Anglo-Saxon type in Scotland.

Some of his successors were familiar enough with Anglo-Saxon and, later, Norman England. Earl Paul, Thorfinn's son, made an application to an Anglo-Norman archbishop, as Queen Margaret did, though he asked not for monks but for a bishop. When Paul's nephew Magnus, the future saint, had a dispute with the Norwegian king, Magnus Barelegs, he went to the court of the king's enemy, the Scottish king Edgar, a vassal of Rufus, the Norman king of England; and later the future saint spent a year at the court of the next Norman king of England, Henry I, Edgar's brother-in-law. Earl Magnus's nephew Rognvald, Earl and Saint, who was brought up in Norway, in his youth visited Grimsby, a place where there was an international trading community. The Orcadian magnate Swein, Asleif's son, is said to have visited King David at Edinburgh, and David communicated directly with Earl Rognvald, whom he directed to protect the 'monks' at Dornoch. One forms the impression of a cosmopolitan society in which men moved easily through Orkney, Scotland and England.

It is therefore difficult to believe that anyone in the twelfth century building a church in Orkney would have proceeded on other than a Norman model in imitation of Durham cathedral and of such Scottish churches as Dunfermline. In 1137 a church on that model and of superlative quality began to rise in Kirkwall, in the shape of the cathedral of St. Magnus, the seat of the bishop of Orkney and Shetland, financed by funds derived from both groups of islands.

VI THE THIRD ROYAL CRUISE: MAGNUS BARELEGS

The reign of Thorfinn 'the Mighty' is always thought of as the apogee of the Orkney earldom, partly because of his achievements within it but largely because he figured on the international stage – not least within the triangular political framework with Norway and Scotland – as none of his predecessors or successors did.

After his death, however, the earldom, though perhaps not yet pruned territorially, was weakened by division between joint heirs and contests between rival claimants. It may well be, too, that 'Scandinavian Scotland' as a whole was beginning to shrink, to the extent that native elements were asserting themselves in the western isles, where so far the development had been parallel to that in Orkney.

Possibly, too, the Scottish king Malcolm Canmore, who had been aggressive enough against England, had been aggressive in the west as well, and even in the north – despite being Thorfinn's son-in-law.

At any rate, when a Norwegian king once more, like Harald Fairhaired or Olaf Trygvasson, determined to show his force in the west, it is evident that he was operating in country that was not effectively part of his dominions and among people who did not consider themselves his subjects or even his friends.

The whole atmosphere suggests hostility: he 'gave quarter' to some, elsewhere he 'plundered and burned', he annexed territory and he had to come to terms with the king of Scots. This time the Norwegian king was Magnus Barelegs.

It was in or about 1098 that he set out, apparently from Oslofjord and not from the west coast. The saga says that he 'came first to the Orkney Islands', which is likely enough if he rounded the Naze and went north to about Stavanger before striking across the sea. From Orkney he proceeded to the Hebrides. The saga mentions Lewis, Uist, Skye, Tiree and Mull in general terms and becomes more specific about other islands.

At the 'holy island' of Iona 'King Magnus came with his host and there gave quarter and peace to all men and to the households of all men. Men say this, that he wished to open the small church of Columcille (Columba); and the king did not go in, but closed the door again immediately, and immediately locked it, and said that none should be so daring thenceforward as to go into this church; and thenceforward it had been so done.' This rather curious episode is parallel to the action of Harald Hardrada, Magnus's grandfather, in locking up St.Olaf's shrine at Trondheim.

The church which Magnus visited at Iona and which was said to have been Columba's five centuries earlier has presumably long disappeared. The oldest church still standing there is St.Oran's Chapel, and even it came in the century after Magnus Barelegs. It seems a little odd that it was thought necessary – or even that it was possible to lock a church on Iona, though it must be said that there had been plenty of reason to lock it against some of Magnus's predecessors.

The saga continues: 'Then King Magnus proceeded with his army south to Islay and plundered there and burned. And when he won that land he set out upon his journey south by Kintyre and plundered there on both sides (starboard and port, Ireland and Scotland). He went everywhere with plundering south as far as Man. Then he proceeded with his host to Wales'. He won a victory at Anglesey and then returned north for his most celebrated exploit – taking a vessel across the isthmus at Tarbert and claiming Kintyre as an island.

From Wales 'King Magnus turned back with his army and proceeded first to Scotland. Then men went between him and Malcolm'. [If the date is right, the king was Edgar, but the fact that the writer put 'Malcolm' may suggest that Malcolm III, now dead for five years, had been well known for taking a militant line in the west.] 'And the kings made peace, to the effect that King Magnus should possess all the islands that lie to the west of Scotland, all between which and the mainland he could go in a ship with the rudder in place. But when King Magnus came north to Kintyre he caused his men to draw a skiff across the isthmus of Kintyre, and to set the rudder in place; the king himself sat in the after-deck, and held the helm. And thus he took possession of the land that then lay to larboard [the south, showing that he had come up the Firth of Clyde and crossed from East Loch Tarbert to the West Loch]. Kintyre is a great land, and better than the best island in the Hebrides, excepting Man. A narrow isthmus is between it and the mainland of Scotland: there long-ships are often drawn across'.

Other accounts tell much the same story about Magnus's operation: e.g., 'His men went into every firth, and all the islands that lay in the firths; and they laid everything under King Magnus, in such manner that they went with their ships between the mainland and the islands, whether they were inhabited or uninhabited'.

Some doubts have been cast on the story of the portage of Tarbert, and it is difficult to believe the tale about Kintyre as if a cession of it to Norway at this point was a novelty, for place-names such as Carradale and Skipness show that the peninsula had been an area of Norse settlement; besides, very soon after this supposed cession the Scottish king believed that Kintyre belonged to him. Perhaps the implication is that there had already been some Scots pressure and Norse withdrawal, and that Scots aggression was soon resumed after Magnus's exploits.

However, not only is there nothing improbable in the exploit of the portage itself, but a little over two centuries later King Robert I (Bruce), who aimed at dominating Argyll from the castle of Tarbert, 'caused his ships to be drawn across the isthmus and because the wind was favourable, he had the sails set. The men of the Isles were utterly dismayed, because an ancient prophecy related that whoever should sail over the isthmus should have the dominion of the Isles'.

While the Tarbert exploit is the most memorable incident in the cruise of King Magnus there was another which had a dual significance. When he

Bishop's Place, Kirkwall, interior (Cathedral tower behind.)

called at Orkney he recruited to his host the young Magnus, grandson of Earl Thorfinn and son of Erlend, who had been joint-earl with his brother Paul. This suggests something like a relationship of dependence between the earl of Orkney and the Norwegian king. Magnus, however, was a reluctant recruit and no fighting man. During the battle off Anglesey he declined to fight against men with whom, he said, he had no quarrel, and he declined equally to get out of the way, but sat on the foredeck singing psalms. That rare bird, a medieval pacifist. He was the future St. Magnus.

King Magnus spent the winter in the Western Isles before returning to Norway next summer. He was back in Orkney and the Hebrides in 1102-3 and was killed in Ireland. He spent more time in the Celtic west than any other Norse king and, if the Hebrideans were already wearing a garment which resembled the belted plaid, or was a forerunner of the kilt, his nickname is explicable as an indication that he conformed to native usage.

VII DECLINE OF NORWEGIAN POWER IN SCOTLAND

If the operations of Magnus Barelegs indicate that before he came on the scene there had been a weakening of Norwegian control in western Scotland, it seems that his expedition did little if anything to halt the process. He evidently dispossessed Godred Crovan, King of Man and the Isles, and made his own son Sigurd king, but within two or three years the throne had been recovered by Olaf, son of Godred, who apparently reigned for fifty years and was succeeded by his son Godred II in 1152.

These rulers appear to have exercised little central control throughout their scattered realm, and leadership in the western isles fell to families bearing Norse names but of mixed race, their homes mainly in the islands and their position based on the sea-power which their ships gave them.

The best known magnate of this type was Somerled (Norse 'summer-voyager'), a son-in-law of King Olaf, who somehow acquired Argyll, in respect of which he owed to the king of Scots an allegiance which was no more than formal and no more effective than the allegiance he owed to the king in Man. In 1154 (apparently in association with a pretender to the Scottish throne) Somerled took up arms against Malcolm IV and in the next three or four years he defeated Godred II, who took refuge in

Norway.

Perhaps as a result of playing off one king against another, he managed to control the greater part of the Isles. He was reconciled to Malcolm in 1160, but in 1164 he led a force of 160 ships, recruited from Ireland and the Hebrides, up the Clyde to Renfrew, where he was killed. Thereupon Godred recovered his throne but probably counted for little in the Hebrides, where the sons of Somerled took over their father's lands, and they have found their places in pedigrees as the progenitors of various MacDonald and Macdougal families. There was little call on them to obey the kings of Scots (even in respect of lands they held on the mainland) and perhaps less to obey the kings of Norway, whether directly or through the Kings of Man. The latter line continued, with some vicissitudes which hardly concern the Scottish historian.

Conditions in the western isles became very disturbed. In 1228-9, we are told, there was 'great dispeace' there: Alan, lord of Galloway, plundered in the Hebrides and Man; Olaf, Godfrey's son, king of Man, held out against Alan, but the 'kings of the Hebrides' (grandsons of Somerled) were not faithful either to him or to King Haakon Haakonsson of Norway. In 1230-31 Norwegians from the islands stormed Bute; Olaf went to Norway, and Haakon appointed as ruler of the Hebrides one Uspak, who, with ships from Norway and Orkney, swept through the islands and into the Firth of Clyde, to join Olaf in renewing the attack on Bute, where Uspak was killed.

Haakon thought himself well served by this expedition, which may have done something to demonstrate his continued interest. It is worth noting that in

King Haakon's Hall and the Rosenkrantz Tower, Bergen.

1238 King Harald I of Man was deprived by Haakon for failing to present himself at the Norwegian court, but after spending two years there he was restored and married a daughter of Haakon. Thus the Norwegian link was maintained.

The earls of Orkney, like Somerled and other chiefs in the west, had to have dealings with more than one sovereign, in Orkney's case the kings of Norway and Scotland. This meant danger as well as opportunity, and in the 1190s the earl of Orkney, Harald Maddadson, found himself like a nut in a nutcracker. He supported a rebellion against King Sverrir of Norway, and on its failure had to surrender to the king, who deprived him of Shetland, which was then ruled by a governor appointed from Norway.

Almost contemporaneously, the earl 'occupied' Moray, bringing on him the wrath of William 'the Lion', to whom also he had to surrender. William proposed that the earl should lose half of Caithness to his cousin Harald the Younger, who proceeded to claim half of the entire earldom but was slain in battle with Maddadson. Maddadson then bargained with William about Caithness and, while he may have failed to recover all of it, he certainly retained at least half of it, to be held of the Scottish crown.

There was another clash in 1222, after Bishop Adam of Caithness was murdered and the Scottish king led a punitive expedition to the diocese. It was about this stage that 'Sutherland' was separated from 'Caithness' and by 1236 it was a separate earldom – a Scottish earldom.

Even Orkney itself, however, was being infiltrated by Scottish influence. It is usually said that the Norse line of jarls ended with John in 1231, but the fact is that both John and his brother and predecessor, David, were at least three-quarters Scots, and their father, Harald Maddadson, had been Scots on the male side. After 1231 the earldom (no longer including Shetland) passed to a series of Scottish families – the Angus line (1231-c.1320), the Strathearn line (1321-57) and finally the St. Clair line (from 1379).

All these earls were Scots or Scoto-Norman in race, their interests were primarily Scottish and some of them may never have set foot in Orkney. As vassals of the Scottish king in respect of Caithness or other property they played their part in Scottish affairs: Magnus, Earl of Caithness and Orkney, was one of the barons in whose name the Declaration of

Arbroath was sent to the Pope in 1320. Shetland, separated as it was from the earldom since 1195, escaped a lot of Scotticisation.

So far as territorial ambitions were concerned, after Caithness and Sutherland were integrated into the Scottish kingdom, attention focused on the west. There were troubles among the descendants of Somerled again in 1248, and once more King Haakon was ready to intervene. Alexander II, who is said to have enforced his authority in mainland Argyll in 1221, set out to attack the islands in 1249 but died on Kerrera.

It could have been seen that the supposed terms of the treaty between Magnus Barelegs and the Scottish crown, whereby the islands went to Norway and the mainland to Scotland, were quite unrealistic: the western seaboard and islands were closely linked by seaborne transport, while the western seaboard was separated from the heart of the Scottish kingdom by mountainous wastes, so that an effective frontier had to be sought not in the narrow western sounds but either in the mountains or in the open ocean. Once Alexander III grew to maturity – he was twenty in 1261 – negotiations began, and money was offered to Haakon for the islands. But Haakon was something of an imperialist, who added Iceland to his dominions and seems to have had a sense (if not delusions) of grandeur; he had no desire to sell off his possessions, and said so.

Relations became increasingly strained: in 1261-2 Haakon forcibly detained Scottish envoys sent to Norway, and raiders from the Scottish mainland burned and slaughtered in Skye. Yet the islands, remote from Haakon's headquarters, might be difficult to retain in the face of determined Scottish pressure, even though they were far from Scottish headquarters too. When Haakon led an expedition into Scottish waters in 1263 he may have been serious in an intention to hold on to his western empire, though it seems unlikely that he intended a serious attack on the heart of Scotland, so far from his base. If he was merely making a demonstration in force to show his muscle it was one that was to prove costly in every sense. The most rational explanation is that he wanted to show that the islands, which must have seemed to be slipping from his grasp, were still at least *de jure* his and that he had something to bargain with, and at the worst he may have reflected that if he made a show of strength he would be in a stronger position should some compromise prove inevitable. At any rate, Norway was not going to lose the islands simply by default.

VIII THE LAST ROYAL CRUISE: HAAKON HAAKONSSON, 1263

There can be few, if any, medieval naval operations about which we have as much detail as we have for the expedition in 1263 of Haakon Haakonsson or Haakon 'the Old', who had been king of Norway 'for forty-six winters' and was now about sixty. The saga account reads almost as if it had been based on a diary or log kept by someone who was present and was in touch with the command. The names are given of dozens of individual Norwegians who sailed with Haakon, and with some at least of them the writer was surely acquainted.

After issuing a general summons at Christmas 1262 he set out on a tour of his kingdom, perhaps to stimulate interest and gather recruits. He evidently started as early as was practicable after the end of winter, for he left Trondheim about the middle of Lent, which would be the end of the first week of March, and went 'by the upper way' (that is, by an inland route) east to Vik (the Oslo area), down to Oslo itself and perhaps to Tönsberg 'and so east to the Elfr'. That may mean that he reached the River Elv, which comes down to the sea north of Gothenburg and was possibly his eastern frontier, but Elv was a common name for a river.

He next went west to Bergen, where he arrived on 3 May and 'proceeded with his preparations as rapidly as possible'. A 'great host', said to have been the largest that ever left Norway, 'collected with him there'. He held 'a general assembly', issued a proclamation 'that he intended to go west beyond the sea with this army to Scotland to avenge the warfare that the Scots had made on his dominions' and he made arrangements for affairs during his absence: two bishops, an abbot, four priests, his 'barons' and other notables and officials were to accompany him, but his son Magnus, who already had the title of king and had in vain offered to lead the expedition in his old father's place, was to govern the country.

'King Haakon had a large ship that he had caused to be built in Bergen, entirely of oak, with 27 [or in other accounts 37] benches; it had a fine dragon's head, all gilded, and so, too, the neck. He had many other large ships, and well equipped'. He sent two messengers to Shetland and the Orkneys, and possibly also to the Hebrides, to engage pilots. The messengers spread the news that the fleet was coming, and this deterred Scots from plundering in the islands as they had been doing. Before leaving Bergen, Haakon sent four ships off in advance and they separated. One arrived in Orkney, but the others sailed 'to the south of Shetland and south west of Thareyiarfjordr [or Barreyiarfjord] and saw no land before Sulnastapi, west from the Orkneys'. There is a Burrafjord in the north of Unst, but the mysterious Thareyiarfjordr may conceivably represent 'Fair Isle Firth', signifying the passage between Shetland and Orkney, and 'Sulnastapi' may be Sule Skerry, which lies almost due west of Birsay in Orkney and north-east of Cape Wrath. These three ships then 'sailed in under Scotland, under Durness, and went ashore there and stormed a certain castle; and the men who were in it fled away. After that they burned more than twenty touns [i.e., settlements]. And then they sailed to the Hebrides and there met Magnus, king of Man'. Possibly Magnus was able to keep his visitors informed as to the extent of his own possessions and save them from spoliation.

After the departure of this advance force, when King Haakon had equipped his ship he put out from Bergen to Eidsvagr but returned to Bergen. Eidsvagr means 'inlet of the isthmus', which is a common name, but an Eidsvåg now within the bounds of Bergen is more likely than one near the mouth of Hardanger Fjord, south of Bergen, or another east of Molde, a long way to the north. On the king's return to Bergen there was a final muster and the fleet moved out to Herdluver.

King Haakon's Hall, Bergen,

'Three nights after Seliamen's festival [St.Sunni-va's Day, 8 July], King Haakon sailed into the North Sea with his whole army ... There was then an excellent wind and fair weather ... Magnus [V], Earl of the Orkneys [1256-75] , went with King Haakon from Bergen, and the king gave him a good longship ... King Haakon got a gentle, favourable wind, and was two nights at sea, and made Shetland with a large part of his army at the place that is called Breideyiar-sund'. This 'broad island sound' is usually taken to have been Bressay Sound, now Lerwick harbour; the suggestion has been made of Uyeasound, and if Haakon proceeded west-about he might have been in the excellent harbour of Brae, sheltered by that admirably broad island of Muckle Roe, but the likelihood is that memory of such an event would endure and it points to Bressay Sound. The saga-writer may quite possibly have been giving his own descriptive names to places, not adopting local usage, and when he writes 'that is called' he may mean 'called by some'.

Wherever the sound was, 'there he lay for nearly half a month. And he sailed from there to the Orkneys, and lay for a while in Ellwick', which is in the island of Shapinsay, opposite Kirkwall. Then he announced to his men that he intended to divide the army, and send part south to the Moray Firth, to plunder there. But he himself sailed to Widewall Bay, in the south-west of South Ronaldsay, and lay there for a time. While he was there he celebrated the Norwegian national festival of St.Olaf's Day (29 July) and entertained some of the local Orcadians, but he also levied a tax on the men of Caithness, for whose support the king of Scots was bidding. 'While King Haakon lay in Widewall Bay, great darkness came upon the sun, in such a way that a small ring was clear about the outside of the sun; and this continued for about an hour of the day'. (There was an annular eclipse of the sun on 5 August.)

On the day of St. Laurence's festival [10 August], King Haakon sailed across the Pentland Firth ... and was off Hvarf [Cape Wrath] and put into the harbour that is called Halseyiarvik'. This place, otherwise As-leifarvik, has not been identified: as it was obviously beyond Cape Wrath, and was an open wick, not a narrow fjord, it can hardly have been Loch Inchard or Loch Laxford (which happens to have its own Norse name, 'Salmon Firth'); it may have been Edrachillis or Enard, but Gruinard might be best. 'Then they sailed to Lewis and on to [South] Rona and then into Skye Sound [i.e., the Sound of Sleat] and to the place called Kerlingarsteinn'. This 'rock of the men, or old men (or women)', was probably Rudha na Caillich, 'the point of the old women', between Loch Alsh and Kyle Rhea; nearby Kyleakin is taken to mean Sound of Haakon, and the name might just possibly pre-serve memory of the visit of the Norwegian king.

Magnus, king of Man, joined the host at this point, followed by Dugald, a king of the Hebrides, but it was becoming evident that Haakon could not rely on all the Hebrideans. A 'King John' declared for Scot-land because he held more land there than in the islands, the rulers of Islay and Kintyre submitted to Haakon only under threat of being plundered, and Kintyre had to pay a tax. On the other hand, there were offers of support from the Irish, who had been suffering at the hands of the English.

It looked as if the restoration of the Norse empire might be more than a dream.

'King Haakon sailed from there to the Sound of Mull and thence under Kerrera ... He divided his army and sent fifty ships, with Kings Magnus and Donald, south to the Mull [or Isthmus] of Kintyre, to plunder there ... Then King Haakon sailed south along Kintyre and lay at the place that is called Gigha'. While he was at Gigha there came 'an abbot of Greyfriars' begging protection, which was granted. In return, his house gave Christian burial to one of Haakon's chaplains, called Simon.' There was no house of Greyfriars anywhere near, and friars did not have abbots; the most likely religious house would be Saddell (Cistercian, white monks), in Kintyre, and Oronsay (Augustinian, black canons), seems less probable.

'That part of the army which the king had sent to the isthmus of Kintyre to plunder,went ashore there and burned the inhabited lands that they found there, and took all the treasure that they could get ... But King Haakon's letter came to them, forbidding them to plunder. Then they went out under Gigha, to King Haakon'. Thus the force was temporarily re-united.

While he was at Kerrera, Haakon, who had already sent some ships ahead to Bute, now 'sent a light ship south to Bute in advance, to those whom he had sent there, because he was long in getting a fair wind. The news was that they had gained a castle [Rothesay] ... The Norwegians who were in Bute went ashore in Scotland and burned a certain village and many touns.' The 'light ship', it may be conjectured, and possibly others, crossed the isthmus at Tarbert, especially as the wind was evidently unfavourable for the

long haul round Kintyre, and went on through the
Kyles of Bute. This would explain a local tradition
that 'King Haakon's galleys' were beached on one of
the isles at the mouth of Loch Ridden.

It is a tiny, rough island, unsuited to support the
larger-than-life tale about 'Haakon's galleys', but one
or two ships, after making a portage at Tarbert, might
well have been there on their way through the Kyles.

When Haakon got his fair wind at last he sailed round
the Mull of Kintyre and put into Lamlash Bay, inside
Holy Island. Messengers came from King Alexander
and there were negotiations; the Scots would not give
up their demand for the islands in the Firth of Clyde,
but may have protracted discussions so as to detain
the Norwegians until the weather deteriorated. 'After
this King Haakon sailed in under the Cumbraes with
the whole army … Then he sent forty ships up Loch
Long [where they made a portage from Arrochar at
the head of Loch Long] to a large lake which is called
Loch Lomond. There are very many islands in that
lake, well inhabited. The Norwegians wasted those
islands with fire. They burned also the dwellings
around the lake, and did the greatest damage… Then
the Norwegians went to their ships [and evidently
returned across to Arrochar and Loch Long] … They
met with a great storm, so that ten ships were
wrecked' and one of their leaders died of disease.
This detachment did not rejoin the main force until
after the action at Largs.

The narrative returns to Haakon in the Firth of Clyde.
'Michaelmas was a Saturday; and on the night of the
Monday following [that is, the night of Sunday-Mon-

day, 30 September – 1 October] a storm came in with fury; and a merchant-ship and long-ships were driven ashore. On the Monday the storm became so violent that some hewed down their masts [to ease strain on the timbers of the hulls], and some drifted. The king's ship drifted up the sound [between Cumbrae and Largs]; it had seven anchors out, and an eighth, a sheet-anchor, but drifted nonetheless. A little later the anchors held. A merchant-ship drifted down on the king's ship and took off the dragon's nostrils, and its anchor caught in the cable of the anchor of the king's ship. Then the anchors of the king's ship began to loosen. Haakon bade them cut the cable of the merchant-ship, which drifted ashore' first on Cumbrae and then on the mainland, where it was looted by Scots. Three or four other ships drove ashore. The Scots – who included 500 armed knights – attacked the stranded Norwegians with arrows, but when Haakon sent a force ashore the Scots fled. There was another action, with the Norwegians outnumbered tenfold, but the Scots were driven off. The Norwegians were able to collect their dead and burn ships which had been driven ashore and were not recoverable.

After the fight, the king sailed back to Lamlash and was rejoined by the Loch Long detachment, but despite the plundering his men had done, provisions were running short and if he was to get back to Norway before winter he could hardly loiter. With little delay he retraced his tracks to Gigha and then out into the Sound of Islay, where he lay for two nights. He made his way out of the Sound on 'the first Sunday in winter' [14 or 21 October] and then met with so great a storm, in pitch darkness, that few ships kept their sails.' The next refuge was in Kerrera Sound or Oban Bay, whence through the familiar Sound of Mull to the Calf of Mull (Calve Island, Tobermory).

The next place mentioned is Rona, east of Skye, again a place visited on the southward voyage; there is no mention of a transit of the Sound of Sleat, but it is unlikely that they made a haul round the west and north of Skye. Setting out from Rona, they were driven by adverse winds to make for 'the West Firth of Skye' or Loch Snizort, where memories of the visit of Haakon's fleet still linger around Kingsburgh.

Northwards again, with a fair wind to carry the fleet round Cape Wrath, but off Durness the wind fell to a dead calm, and they put into 'Goafjord', perhaps Loch Eriboll, where they were on 27-28 October. Then conditions became more favourable and on 29 October the king sailed into Osmundwall or Kirk Hope in Hoy, the scene of the encounter of his prede-cessor Olaf Trygvasson with Earl Sigurd nearly two centuries before, and then across to Widewall Bay in South Ronaldsay. One ship was lost in the Pentland Firth; another, swept on by a westerly wind, nar-rowly escaped being driven into the whirlpool called the Swelkie, off Stroma, but 'by God's mercy was driven eastward into the open sea' and reached Nor-way.

Despite that westerly wind, conditions were thought unfavourable for the whole fleet to attempt a home-ward voyage, and Haakon decided to winter in Ork-ney, with twenty ships and his 'barons'. After All Saints' day (1 November) he caused his own ship to sail to 'Midland's Haven', presumably between Midland's Ness and Orphir, and some ships were laid up there, others at Scapa, which was only two miles, across a narrow isthmus, from Kirkwall, which was obviously to be the king's headquarters. He rode out to Midland's Haven on 10 November, by which time he was very ill.

He remained on his ship for the night, but next day, which was Sunday, he heard Mass ashore. Then he gave orders for his ship to be laid up and bade men take great pains in looking after all the ships.

Returning to Scapa, Haakon rode across to Kirkwall, where he arranged for the billeting of his men. He himself settled in the bishop's palace, taking his meals not in the hall but in his own chambers on an upper storey. After lying for some nights he was somewhat better and was on his feet for three days. On the third day he visited the shrine of St. Magnus in the cathedral nearby. As it was time to prepare himself physically as well as spiritually for death, he had a bath prepared for him and went into it and had himself shaved.

The same night, growing worse, he took to bed again. He had the Bible, in Latin, read to him, but he found it difficult to understand and instead he had Norwegian books read night and day – first stories of holy men and when those came to an end the series of the kings of Norway, one after another. When the series of the kings had been read, down to Sverri (1184-1217), he made them begin to read Sverri's saga.

It was then read constantly, both night and day, whenever he was awake. He provided for the payment of war-wages to his body-guard and determined that a mark of refined silver should be given to each guardsman and half a mark to the royal retainers and the torch-bearers... Then also letters were written to king Magnus regarding the government of the land and about the other affairs in which King Haakon wished to assist his subjects.

'He received extreme unction one night before St.Lucia's mass' [that is, Wednesday-Thursday, 12-13 December]. He was then still able to speak. His confidants asked him if he had another son surviving, besides King Magnus to whom they could turn if things should go so badly that they should lose him or King Magnus; and he said emphatically that it was not so.

'On the Saturday following, late in the evening, the king's sickness so pressed upon him that he lost the power of speech. And when midnight had passed Almighty God called Haakon from this world's life. After his death a requiem was sung. Then men went away from the apartment, everyone except Bishop Thorgils [of Stavanger] and Bryniolf, John's son, and two other men. They washed the body and did for it all the other services that were fitting for so famous a lord and chief.

'On the Sunday the king's body was carried into the loft-hall and set upon a bier. The body was clothed in robes of state and a garland was set upon his head, and in all respects things were done as they ought to have been done for a crowned king. Then the people went in to see the body; and it seemed to men bright and well-favoured and with a fair redness in the countenance, as of a living man. It was a great consolation to men in the great grief that had then fallen upon them to see so fair a corpse of the departed man and of their lord. The bodyguard watched over the body during the night.

'On Tuesday the body was laid in a coffin and he was buried in Magnus's church, in the choir. At Yule, the bishop and Andrew Plyttr provided as the king had determined and to all men good pay was given.' After temporary interment in Kirkwall, the body was taken to Bergen for burial in the cathedral. The Saga did not represent Haakon as a failure: 'He had won back again all the dominions that King Magnus Barelegs had acquired'.

The decisive event of 1263 was not anything which happened at Largs but the withdrawal of the Norwegians and the death of their warlike old monarch. The sequel, in the shape of Scottish negotiations with Haakon's son and successor, Magnus V, leading to the treaty of Perth whereby in 1266 Norway ceded the western isles, is well known, but flavour is given to both the battle and its sequel by the words of the Chronicle of Melrose, which show how contemporary Scots saw it. There was national conceit, pride in the house of Melrose and an almost naive belief in Providence – all hard to reconcile with a claim to be 'meek'; and the chronicler was dismissive about the 'little islands' of the Hebrides. The Norwegians presented Largs as a successful rearguard action to recover their stranded ships, but the Scots saw it as a famous victory over invaders.

IX THE TREATY OF PERTH, 1266: CESSION OF THE HEBRIDES

The decisive event of 1263 was not anything which happened at Largs but the withdrawal of the Norwegians and the death of their warlike old monarch. The sequel, in the shape of Scottish negotiations with Haakon's son and successor, Magnus V, leading to the treaty of Perth whereby in 1266 Norway ceded the western isles, is well-known, but flavour is given to both the battle and its sequel by the words of the Chronicle of Melrose, which show how contemporary Scots saw it.

There was national conceit, pride in the house of Melrose and an almost naive belief in Providence – all hard to reconcile with a claim to be 'meek'; and the chronicler was dismissive about the 'little islands' of the Hebrides. The Norwegians presented Largs as a successful rearguard action to recover their stranded ships, but the Scots saw it as a famous victory over invaders.

MELROSE CHRONICLE

'1263. Haco, king of Norway, with a great force of ships, came by the west sea to do battle with the king of Scotland. But indeed, as Haco himself affirmed, he was repelled not by human strength but by divine power, which shattered his ships and inflicted disease on his army; moreover, those who on the third day after Michaelmas [2 October] came to give battle were defeated and overthrown by the horse and foot of the land; wherefore they were compelled to board their ships again with their dead and wounded and so to return to their native land more shamefully than they had come.

'This year [1263/4], on St. Agnes's day [21 January], the queen of Scotland bore a son; ... whence it happened that on the same day when it was announced to the king of Scotland that a son had been given to him by God it was announced to him that the king of Norway had died; wherefore, transported by a double joy, he gave thanks to God, who exalts the meek and humbles the proud...

'1265. There was sent to Norway, by King Alexander III, Reginald of Roxburgh, a monk of Melrose, a man of glorious eloquence and most excellent counsel, to obtain the land of Man, formerly called a kingdom, with the little islands lying around it'. Opinion among the Norwegian magnates was divided, but the outcome of discussion was that the islands should be sold. 'Therefore a treaty was made between the two kings that the king of Scotland should pay 100 merks sterling to the king of Norway in perpetuity for recognition of homage due to the king of Norway by the said Alexander; and that 4000 merks in one sum should be paid for the islands to the king of Norway, to be received by him in Orkney by the hands of the bishop of Orkney.

'1266. Reginald returned from Norway after carrying out the business for which he had been sent. No one out of the sons of the Scots could have achieved this except the said monk, with his wisdom and eloquence, who deserved for his house the grace and favour for ever of the kings of Scotland, unless they are found ungrateful and render evil for good to

"Anno Domini MCCLXIII. Haco rex Norwagie cum copiosa navium multitudine venit per mare occidentale ad debellandum regem Scotie. Sed re vera, ut ipse H. affirmbat, non eum repulit vis humana sed virtus divina, que naves ejus confregit et [in] exercitum suum mortalitatem inmisit; insuper, eos qui tercia die post sollempnitatem Sancti Michaelis ad preliandum convenerant, per pedissequos patrie debellavit atque prostravit. Quapropter coacti sunt cum vulneratis et mortuis suis naves sua[s] repetere, et sic turpius quam venerant repatriare. Hoc anno in die Sancti Agnetis, apud Gedewrth peperit regina Scotie filium, quem, a Gamelino episcopo Sancti Andree baptizatum, juxta patris imperium vocaverunt Alexandrum; unde contigit ut eodem die quo nuntiatum est regi Scotie filium a Deo sibi esse datum, nuntiaretur ei et regem Norwagie defunctum; quapropter dupplici gaudio exhillaratus, gratias reddidit Deo, qui humiles exaltat et superbos humiliat."

Melrose Chronicle on the Battle of Largs; facsimile and transcript the house of Melrose, which God avert from the heart of every Christian king! The monk was followed to Scotland by the chancellor of the king of Norway, bringing the treaty mentioned above'.

The terms of the treaty differ in some details from what is stated in the Chronicle and they enlarge in a very enlightened way on the rights of the inhabitants of the islands:

TREATY OF PERTH

'The agreement ... for a settlement of the ... disputes of the isles of Man and the Sudreys ... was made ... between ... Magnus, ... king of Norway, by his solemn envoys, compearing there, ... and ... Alexander, ... king of Scots, personally compearing there with the clergy and greater magnates of his realm:

'That ... Magnus, king of Norway, ... granted, resigned and quit-claimed ... for himself and his heirs for ever, Man with the rest of the Sudreys and all other islands on the west and south of the great sea ... ; the said islands to be held ... by the said lord Alexander ... and his heirs, ... with the right of patronage of the bishopric of Man (saving ... the right, jurisdiction and liberty of the church of Nidaros ...), excepting the islands of Orkney and Shetland, which the said king of Norway has reserved specially to his dominion ...; in such wise that the men of the said islands which are ceded ... shall be subject to the laws and customs of the realm of Scotland; ... if they should wish to remain in the said islands under the lordship of the said king of Scots they may remain in his dominion freely and in peace, but if they desire to retire they may do so, with their goods ... so that they be not compelled either to remain or to retire contrary to the laws and customs of the realm of Scotland and their own will.

'Therefor the foresaid lord Alexander ... and his heirs ... shall give and render for ever to the said king of Norway and his heirs and their assignees within the octave of the nativity of St. John the Baptist, in Orkney, that is, in the land of the lord king of Norway, in the church of St.Magnus, into the hand of the bishop of Orkney or the bailie of the said lord king of Norway hereto specially deputed by him, or ... shall deposit in the said church ... (for the use of the said lord king of Norway) ... the sum of 100 merks good and lawful sterling money ... and also 4000 merks sterling ... within the next four years at place and term foresaid, namely 1000 merks in the octave of the nativity of St. John the Baptist in the year of grace 1267, with 100 merks of the foresaid annual, and in the year of grace 1268 at the same place and time 1000 merks and 100 merks of the foresaid annual [and likewise for 1269 and 1270, after which the 100 merks of annual only] ...

'If it happen ... that the men of the king of Norway suffer shipwreck in the kingdom or dominion of the king of Scotland or contrariwise, it shall be lawful for them freely and quietly to gather their ships, broken or shattered, along with all their goods, and to have them, to sell and to dispose of them, without any claim, as long as they have not abandoned them. And if anyone acts contrary to this act of common agreement concerning these goods or ships, fraudulently or violently abstracting from them, and is convicted thereof, let him be punished as a plunderer and breaker of the peace as he deserves.'

This treaty marked the beginning of a lasting peace

between the two kingdoms. Fifteen years after the treaty was made, and no doubt with the intention of ensuring stability in Scoto-Norwegian amity, Margaret, the daughter of Alexander III, married Erik of Norway, who had just succeeded his father Magnus on the Norwegian throne.

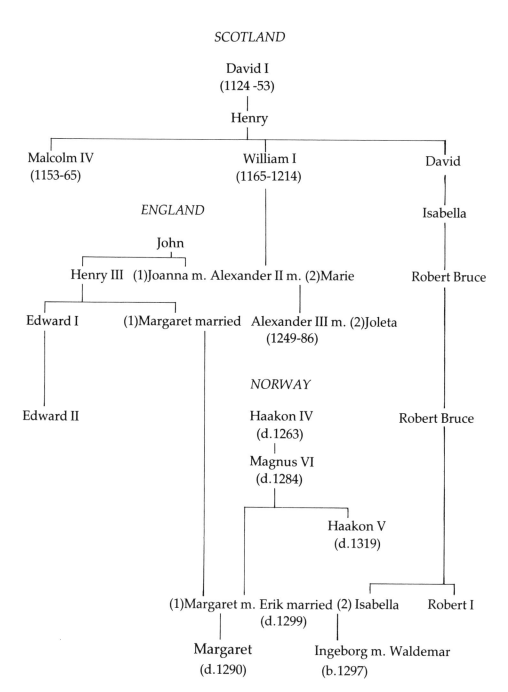

SCOTLAND

David I
(1124 -53)
|
Henry

Malcolm IV   William I   David
(1153-65)   (1165-1214)

ENGLAND   Isabella

John

Henry III (1)Joanna m. Alexander II m. (2)Marie Robert Bruce

Edward I (1)Margaret married Alexander III m. (2)Joleta
             (1249-86)

          NORWAY

Edward II   Haakon IV   Robert Bruce
         (d.1263)
         Magnus VI
         (d.1284)

            Haakon V
            (d.1319)

(1)Margaret m. Erik married (2) Isabella Robert I
      (d.1299)

Margaret   Ingeborg m. Waldemar
(d.1290)   (b.1297)

X THE MAID OF NORWAY

The king sits in Dunfermline town
   Drinking the blude-red wine;
'O whar will I get a skeely skipper
   To sail this new ship o' mine?'
Our king has written a braid letter
   And sealed it with his hand
And sent it to Sir Patrick Spens,
   Was walking on the strand.
'To Noroway, to Noroway,
   To Noroway o'er the faem;
The king's daughter o' Noroway,
   'Tis thou must bring her hame'.

An expedition was indeed sent to bring to
Scotland the daughter of a king of Norway, not
once but on three occasions, and the ballad may
represent a confused intermingling of elements from
more than one of them.

It certainly does not agree with the historical facts
relating to the 'Maid of Norway'; the expedition to
fetch her was not commissioned by a king and, while
the voyage ended in tragedy, the disaster was not
shipwreck. Perhaps the most instructive stanza in the
ballad is one which indicated an awareness in
Scotland that Norway was not a very distant country;

They hoysed their sails on Monenday morn
   Wi' a' the speed they may;
They hae landed in Noroway
   Upon a Wodensday.

In the thirteenth century the connections of the
Scottish royal family with the English ruling lines
were very close, for Alexander II (1214–49) and his
son Alexander III (1249–86) had each taken an English
princess as his first wife, so that both of those Scottish
kings were the brothers-in-law of their English
contemporaries, Henry III and Edward I.

But Scottish connections with the Norwegian
monarchy were likewise close. King Erik of Norway,
grandson of Haakon Haakonsson, was married to
Margaret, daughter of Alexander III, and after she
died he took as his second wife Isabella Bruce, sister
of the Robert Bruce who became King Robert I.

Margaret, the Maid of Norway, was the daughter
of King Erik, who succeeded his father Magnus in
1280, by his first wife, the Scottish princess Margaret,
whom he married in 1281. Their daughter Margaret
was born within two years of the marriage, and her
mother, Queen Margaret, died at Tönsberg, on the
west side of Oslofjord, on 9 April 1283. The Scottish
king Alexander III, the Maid's grandfather, had two
sons, but one died in 1281 and the other early in 1284,
leaving as heir to the Scottish throne Alexander's
granddaughter, the infant Margaret.

When her parents had married, the right of their
sons or daughters to succeed to the Scottish throne
had been recognised. It is a measure of the sense of
crisis that within days of the death of Alexander's
remaining son in 1284, the Scottish magnates as-

sembled to acknowledge Margaret's right to succeed should Alexander III have no other children.

Alexander III did marry again, in October 1285, but in the darkness of the night of 19 March 1286 he was killed when he fell over the cliffs east of Burntisland as he rode from Edinburgh to join his wife at King- horn. There seemed no alternative for the Scots but to acknowledge his granddaughter Margaret as their Queen. There were, however, grave doubts about the possibility or propriety of having a female – espe- cially a little girl no more than three years old – reigning in her own right.

Many thought a king preferable to a queen, and some descendants of earlier kings thought that it would be better for one of them to succeed rather than bring over this child from Norway.

It is a familiar story that Edward I of England, who was the child's great-uncle, proposed to continue the series of marriages between the Scottish and English royal families, and the Scots agreed that Margaret should be betrothed to the Prince of Wales, after- wards Edward II, who was about a year younger than she was. This seemed to many in both countries a splendid chance to bring about a peaceful union of England and Scotland – three hundred years before the 'Union of the Crowns' which took place in 1603. Besides, Margaret's prospective father-in-law, Ed- ward I, could be relied on to support her position against challenges in Scotland.

King Erik had of course to give his consent to his daughter's betrothal to the English prince, and there is no reason to think that he was at all reluctant, but possibly the prospective father-in-law, Edward of

England, was more enthusiastic and perhaps unduly eager to get the girl into his own hands. At any rate, Edward took it upon himself to fit out and despatch an English ship to bring Margaret across the sea, and saw to the provision of tempting delicacies like rice, sturgeon, ginger and whalemeat for the child-queen, now between seven and eight years old.

The ship came back within a month, without the princess and with eleven sailors sick or dead. Edward may well have been first in the field, but Norway and Scotland were also eager for the responsibility – or the privilege – of bringing the child-queen across the sea. The Norwegian king possibly protested, perhaps with some indignation, that he had ships of his own, and it was in a Norwegian vessel that The Maid set out for Scotland in September 1290. But the 'Guardians' who were ruling Scotland had made their own bid:

> Thai ordanyd message to send sune
> Oure se in till Norway
> In till Scotland till bring that May
> The Kyng of Norwayis douchter fayre
> Off Scotland and Norway that tyme ayre ...
> To this passage thai ordanyd then
> Honorabill knychtis and gret men;
> Dwelland in to Fyiffe war twa ...
> Off the Wemys Schir Dawy
> Schir Mychel Scot of Balwery
> Thai ware twa well commendyt men.

So says the chronicler Wyntoun (who, as a canon of St.Andrews and prior of Lochleven, had local knowledge of Fife). Others name the Wemyss laird 'Michael'. A silver basin still preserved at Wemyss

Castle is alleged to be a relic of this mission.

The plan had evidently been that Margaret should land in Orkney, where she would be handed over by her Norwegian guardians to representatives of the Scottish government and in the presence also of English representatives, who were on their way to Orkney in September and had reached Wick when they learned that there had been a disaster. It is a fair conjecture that equinoctial gales in the North Sea proved too much for the little girl. She died about 26 September, either off the coast of Orkney or ashore in the islands.

Margaret, we are told, expired 'between the hands of Bishop Narve of Bergen and in the presence of the best men who had followed her from Norway'. It is moving to think of the little girl, around whom so many hopes and so many schemes had focused, dying surrounded by dignified but desperately worried men.

The reaction in Scotland is described in a remarkable letter written at Leuchars on 7 October 1290 by William Fraser, Bishop of St. Andrews and the leading churchman in Scotland, to Edward I, to whom he naturally appealed as the brother-in-law of the late King Alexander and as great-uncle and prospective father-in-law of the Maid. Fraser's words suggest vividly and movingly how rumour and counter-rumour swept Scotland and how there was something like panic with the prospect of disputed succession to the throne and the likelihood of civil war among various claimants, especially John Balliol and Robert Bruce, both descended from a younger brother of William I.

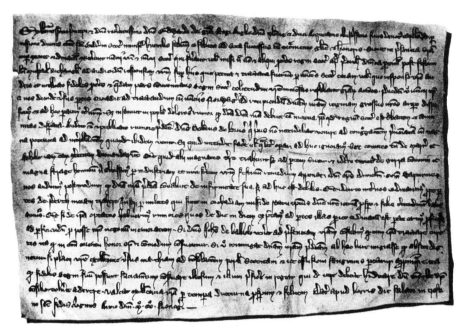

Letter of Bishop William Fraser to Edward I, 1290.

Later historians, who always like to be on the winning side, have favoured the claims of Bruce, but Fraser clearly regarded him as a disturbing influence and advised Edward to enter into negotiations with Balliol.

Fraser opened by explaining to Edward that English and Scottish representatives had met at Perth on 1 October to continue discussions, no doubt over some of the details planned for The Maid's future life. He proceeded:

'Your ambassadors and we set ourselves to hasten our steps towards Orkney to confer with the ambassadors of Norway for receiving our Lady the Queen, and for this we had prepared our journey. But there sounded through the people a sorrowful rumour that our said Lady was dead, on which account the kingdom of Scotland is disturbed and the community distracted'.

Then enters the sinister Bruce, who had been waiting in the wings: 'And the said rumour being heard and published, Sir Robert de Brus, who before did not intend to come to the foresaid meeting, came with a great following to confer with some who were there. But what he intends to do or how to act as yet we know not. But the Earls of Mar and Atholl are already collecting their army and some of the nobles of the land are won over to their party, and on that account there is fear of a general war and a great slaughter of men, unless the Highest, by means of your industry and good service, apply a speedy remedy'.

At that point the bishop seems to have paused, while a fresh rumour came in...

'My lords the Bishop of Durham, Earl Warenne and I heard afterwards that our foresaid Lady recovered of her sickness, but she is still weak. And therefore we have agreed to remain about Perth until we have certain news by the knights who are sent to Orkney about the condition of our Lady – would that it may be prosperous and happy. If we have the reports which we wish concerning her and which we await from day to day, we will be ready to set out for those parts [Orkney] as is ordained, for carrying out the business committed to us, to the best of our power'.

Reflecting further on the gloomy prospects for Scotland and the hope which lay in Edward, the Bishop went on:

'If Sir John de Balliol comes to your presence we advise you to take care so to treat with him that in any event your honour and advantage be preserved'. Then he switched back to the main thought in his mind and concluded with a suggestion that, 'if it turn out that our foresaid Lady has departed this life (may it not be so), let your excellency deign if you please to approach the Border, for the consolation of the Scottish people and for saving of the shedding of blood, so that the faithful men of the kingdom may keep their oath inviolate and set over them for King him who of right ought to have the succession if so be that he will follow your counsel. May your excellency have long life and health, prosperity and happiness.'

The sequel in Scotland is well known. There was no immediate and obvious successor, and no less than thirteen competitors put in claims. One of the claimants was King Erik, the girl's father. There was nothing ridiculous in this, for, as he was his daughter's heir in private law, why should he not be heir to her throne as well? The choice fell on John Balliol, who in modern terms had the best right, for his grandmother was the elder sister of Bruce's mother.

King Erik, widowed by the death of his first wife, married again, and by his second wife once more had a daughter and no son. As Norwegian law then stood, a female should not succeed, and when Erik died in 1299 the Norwegian throne went to his brother Haakon. At that point Erik's surviving daughter was only two years old, and the choice of Haakon in preference to such an infant is understandable.

But had his elder daughter, Margaret, still been alive she would by this time have been about sixteen and might well have been thought quite a suitable person to be queen. (In 1302 the law was modified to allow females to succeed.) Had The Maid, at her father's death, been the wife of the heir to the English throne, as had been the intention, that might or might not have been an additional reason for taking seriously any right she had to the Norwegian succession. Wyntoun, perhaps as a patriotic Scot anxious to magnify his own royal line, called Margaret 'off Scotland and Norway that tyme ayre' and wrote that she 'apperyd till have bene be the lawch of Norway quene'. There must have been those who supported her claim to a place in the Norwegian succession.

It is an intriguing thought that there might have been a triple union of crowns – Scotland, England, Norway – when Edward II succeeded his father in 1306. (It was to come about before the end of the century that another Margaret was Queen of Norway, Denmark and Sweden.)

The Maid's body was taken back to Norway, where her father insisted on having the coffin opened so that he could satisfy himself of the identity of the corpse. This did not prevent the appearance several years later of a woman who claimed to be the Maid, and in 1301 she was put to death in Bergen by burning and her husband was beheaded. Margaret was buried in the old cathedral of Bergen, where the relics of St. Sunniva were preserved.

That cathedral has long been demolished, but on its site, in an open space behind Haakonshallen, the hall built by her great-grandfather Haakon Haakonsson, there is a memorial bearing on one side a list of the names of the sovereigns of Norway who were crowned in the building and on another side the names of the royal persons who were buried in it. The last three names on the second list read:

1263 KONG HAAKON HAAKONSSON
1283 DRONNING MARGARETA ALEXANDERSDATTER
1290 JOMFRU MARGARETA EIRIKSDATTER

They are known to us as Haakon the Old, who fought at Largs in 1263, the Princess Margaret, daughter of Alexander III of Scotland, who married King Erik, and Margaret, our 'Maid of Norway'. There is no better place to recall the interaction of the Scottish and Norwegian pasts and to reflect on one of the 'might have beens' of history.

There seems a faint possibility that a place might be found for Sir Patrick Spens at an earlier stage in the Maid's story. In the crisis of 1284, when the death of

Plaque on the site of Christ's Church, the old cathedral; of Bergen, naming the royal persons buried there.

Prince Alexander left the king of Scots without a
surviving child and the Maid became heir, did King
Alexander impulsively decide to send to Norway for
the infant? If so, 'Sir Patrick Spens' might have been
chosen to play the part which the Guardians assigned
in 1290 to those two Fife lairds Wemyss and Balwea-
rie.

XI SCOTLAND'S INDEPENDENCE MAINTAINED: NORWAY'S LOST

The survival of the Maid and her marriage to Edward II would have led to the merging of the Scottish kingdom in a union where it could have been only a junior partner.

After the death of the Maid, the accession of John Balliol to the throne of Scotland as a vassal of England meant subordination to England, against which Balliol rebelled, only to bring conquest on his kingdom by Edward I (1296) and his own deposition. Resistance was maintained intermittently, at first unsuccessfully by William Wallace (1297-8) and later, with ultimate success, by Robert Bruce, grandson of the claimant of 1290, in a series of campaigns which began in 1306 and included the victory of Bannockburn in 1314.

The Norwegian connection figured more than once in the story. In 1295, when the ambitious Edward I, who had recently conquered Wales, was threatening France as well as Scotland, France made two treaties of mutual assistance, one with Norway and the other with Scotland. The sister of Robert Bruce, the future king, had in 1292 been married to King Erik, whose previous marriage had been to Alexander III's daughter. Who took the initiative in planning his second marriage we do not know, but it looks as if the Norwegians, after having had a link with the Scottish reigning line were not averse from maintaining a connection through a marriage with a family who had prospects of the Scottish throne.

Bruce, on his side, clearly kept his Norwegian in-laws in mind. When, immediately after he had claimed the crown in 1306, disaster befell him in the battle of Methven, near Perth, his queen and her ladies headed northward and they may have been hoping to reach Orkney and perhaps Norway when they were captured by the English at Tain. Shortly afterwards, when King Robert himself disappeared from the Scottish scene, he may have proceeded north from the western isles to Orkney, still a Norwegian dependency, or even to Norway itself. To have done so might have been more profitable than studying spiders in Rathlin, the activity with which he is usually credited at that stage in his career.

Once Bruce had returned to Scotland and made sufficient headway against the English to deserve recognition, he concluded the treaty of Inverness with Norway in 1312. Erik, his brother-in-law, had died in 1299, and the treaty was made with Erik's brother, Haakon V.

This treaty is the first one between Scotland and Norway of which the original survives among the Scottish records, for although we have the text of the treaty of Perth of 1266 the original parchment is not extant. The 1312 treaty recited the terms of that of 1266, which both parties solemnly reaffirmed. All else apart, this was a reminder (by one side) or an admission (by the other) of the Scottish obligation to pay the 100 merks due each year as the Annual of Norway, but the representatives of both kingdoms, while at Inverness, dealt with a number of grievances arising from depredations by Scots in Orkney and the arrest of Scots merchants in Norway.

Two years after the treaty of Inverness, King Robert was victorious at Bannockburn. Other campaigns followed, mainly by Scots invading England, until the English, in 1328, acknowledged Bruce as king of an independent Scotland. That was by no means the end of the struggle, for within a few years the English again planted a vassal – Edward Balliol, son of King John – on the Scottish throne, and Bruce's young son David had to take refuge for a time in France.

Not only so, but war between Scotland and England went on intermittently until 1560 and the Scots suffered many heavy defeats, but Bannockburn had shown that the English could be defeated, and in spite of all reverses Scotland remained unconquered. (It must be said that west highlanders, who had been subjects of the king of Norway until 1266, had only limited enthusiasm for the cause of Scottish independence and not infrequently supported England against the kings of Scots.)

When union with England came about it did so peacefully through the marriage of James IV to the English princess Margaret in 1503 and the consequent accession of James VI to the English throne in 1603 (which meant two kingdoms under a single monarch) and, in 1707, the creating of a United Kingdom in terms of a Treaty of Union freely agreed between the two countries.

The fortunes of Norway were different. That country

seems in the middle of the fourteenth century to have suffered with quite exceptional severity from the Black Death, which greatly reduced the population and led to a kind of economic and perhaps moral anaemia. Yet the political fate of the country was, like Scotland's, shaped largely by royal marriages. Haakon V, who concluded the treaty of Inverness, left only a daughter, who married Erik of Sweden and whose son Magnus united the crowns of Norway and Sweden for a short time; the next king of Norway was Haakon VI, who married Queen Margaret of Denmark, and in 1397 the Union of Kalmar joined the three kingdoms.

The Swedes were restive and soon recovered their independence but the union of Norway with Denmark continued until 1814, followed by a union with Sweden which lasted until 1905. By that time Scotland had been united with England for two centuries.

From the late fourteenth century, therefore, Scotland was no longer concerned at a political level with an independent Norwegian kingdom; its political and diplomatic dealings were with Norway-Denmark, which meant in practice with Denmark. Such dealings figured prominently in Scottish international activity; it surprises some people to learn from the published *Letters of James IV* that the number of letters the king of Scots exchanged with the king of Denmark slightly exceeded the number he exchanged with the king of France.

At economic and cultural levels Denmark had its own very close links with Scotland. In this connection it must be remembered that, although Sweden ceased to be even nominally under the same crown as

Denmark in the early sixteenth century, Denmark continued until the mid-seventeenth century to include what is now the southmost part of Sweden, which meant that Denmark straddled the entrance to the Baltic and, from the fortresses of Kronborg at Helsingör and Kärnan at Hälsingborg, controlled traffic in and out of that sea.

Towns like Malmö, Lund and Landskrona were then in Denmark and they, as well as Helsingör and Copenhagen on the western side of the Sound, were focal points for Scottish traders, many of whom settled in those continental ports and played prominent parts in their affairs. A recent book by Thomas Riis, *Should Auld Acquaintance be forgot?* is an exhaustive study of Scoto-Danish relations between about 1450 and 1700, with massive lists of Scots who were in Denmark in that period.

What may be called the heroic, or perhaps imperialist, phase of Norwegian history may be said to have ended with Haakon Haakonsson; it must be said that the Danish crown, absorbed in continental politics and its relations with the Hanseatic League, did not look west over seas as Norwegian kings had done, so that the North Atlantic Empire was neglected. The Greenland settlements died out and Iceland and Faroe sank into a depression which lasted for centuries.

Yet, as a result of the dynastic union with Norway, Denmark acquired or inherited an important link with Scotland in the shape of the 'Annual of Norway' – or rather the right to it, for it seems seldom to have been paid. This payment in respect of the western isles of Scotland came to be tied up with the question of the future of the northern isles.

XII THE TRANSFER OF ORKNEY AND SHETLAND, 1468-72

It is among the most picturesque and therefore best remembered events in Scottish history that King Christian I of Denmark and Norway, unable to raise the 60,000 florins of the Rhine which he had promised as the dowry of his daughter, Margaret, on her marriage to James III, King of Scots, pledged his lands and rights in Orkney for 50,000 florins in 1468 and his lands and rights in Shetland for a further 8,000 florins in the following year.

But these transactions were no more than incidents in a long process whereby the islands were gradually transferred from Norwegian control and were stage by stage incorporated into the Scottish kingdom. They did not in themselves mean an abrupt substitution of Scottish rule and Scots law for Norwegian rule and Norse law.

It is not often remembered that a clause of the agreement of 1468 finally extingushed, after more than two centuries, the Annual of Norway, that ancient liability of Scotland to pay 100 merks yearly in respect of the western isles, ceded by Norway in 1266. And it is very seldom recalled that a treaty of 1281 arranging the marriage of Alexander III's daughter to Erik of Norway provided that, should the Norwegians not fulfil the terms, then Orkney was to be ceded to Scotland; the possibility of such a cession had thus been envisaged two hundred years before 1468.

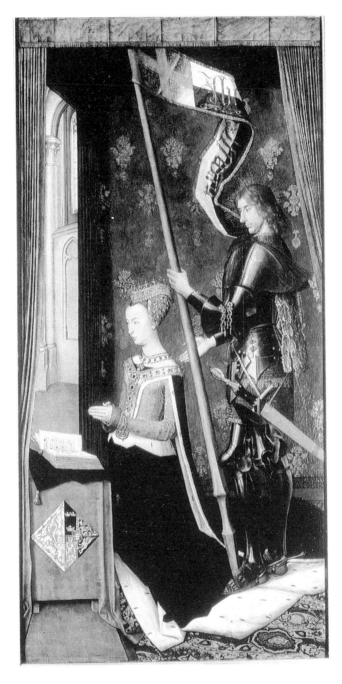

MARGARET, *Princess of Denmark and Norway, married James III in*
Holyroodhouse, 1469. Trinity College Altarpiece

In 1460, when the possibility of a marriage of Princess Margaret to James III was first discussed, the Scots proposed that to make up her dowry the Annual of Norway should be extinguished and Orkney and Shetland should be ceded. Thus the transfer of Orkney and Shetland in 1468-9 did not reflect a wholly novel idea. Besides, long before 1468 Scottish influence had been infiltrating the islands. Since before 1200 the earldom of Orkney had been held by men who were partly of Scottish blood and since 1231 it had been in the hands of families whose interests were largely Scottish and who were vassals of the Scottish king in respect of properties in the south. Such earls can have done nothing to strengthen or even maintain the connection with Norway.

It is true that the formal superiority of the kings of Norway over the earls of Orkney, Scots though they now were, was maintained, but there were indications that provisions designed to ensure that Orkney did not in practice slip altogether out of the Norwegian grasp were becoming ineffective. Whereas in 1389, when Norwegian councillors defined the succession to the crown, the name of the Earl of Orkney appeared second on the list, in 1448 there was no Orcadian representative present at the inauguration ceremonies of the Norwegian king.

Then in 1460 and in 1461, when the earl was summoned to do homage in person to King Christian, he made excuses and there seems to be no evidence that he ever did homage. From time to time, when the earldom was vacant, the king had taken it into his own hands but even then it was Scots, not Norwe-

gians, who administered it in his name. It even
appears that already before 1468 the king was finding
it impossible to collect revenues due to him from the
islands and could no longer make his authority
effective in this distant dependency. Shetland was
not far from Bergen; it was a long way from
Copenhagen.

Scottish influence in the islands was growing not
only in the secular sphere but also in the church,
despite its continued dependence on the archbishopric of Trondheim. Four years after the first St. Clair
was appointed to the earldom a member of his family
became bishop, and there followed a series of Scottish bishops, latterly Thomas Tulloch and then William Tulloch (who was keeper of the privy seal of
Scotland and an active figure at the Scottish court).
Church appointments provided a channel for the
infiltration of Scots even into Shetland, which was to
some extent sheltered from Scotticisation in the secular field; the archdeaconry of Shetland, like the bishopric, passed into the hands of Tullochs – three of
them in succession.

The Scots who filled the leading positions in church
and state brought their kinsmen and clients in their
train. In the 1420s the Orcadians were complaining of
oppression by 'foreigners' and it is evident that there
must have been a substantial Scottish immigration
before 1468, to produce a fair number of officials and
landowners. The latest extant Orkney document in a
Scandinavian tongue is dated as early as 1426 and
even that was composed in official Norwegian and
not in the local Norn. Ten years after that the lawman
of Orkney was writing in Lowland Scots. It was diffe-

rent in Shetland, where the latest document in Norwegian belongs to so late as 1607.

So much had happened before 1466 and so many Scots had established themselves in Orkney that the king of Denmark can hardly have thought that the effective reintegration of the islands within his dominions was practicable. What happened in 1466 was not the relinquishing of an integral part of the Norwegian kingdom. But what did happen in 1468 and 1469? The treaties specified 'our lands of the islands of Orkney' and 'our lands of the islands of Shetland', with 'all and sundry rights, services and rightful pertinents belonging to us by royal right'.

Crown lands clearly had first place, and there were assuredly lands in Orkney which belonged to the crown; we know less about crown lands in Shetland, and if royal estates were less extensive there that might explain the 8000 merks for Shetland as against 50,000 for Orkney, for although Orkney is far more fertile, the area of Shetland is about half as much again as that of Orkney. The negotiators were not necessarily thinking very precisely of comparative valuations. Besides lands which were in the king's hands, there were lands of which the king was landlord or superior, and rents or other dues from them would be included. Among other crown revenues, there were fines or other profits of justice, and also taxes.

Crown rights should have included a voice in the choice of bishops, the patronage of other ecclesiastical benefices and the enjoyment of the temporalities of bishoprics during vacancies.

There was no specific clause now about the bishopric as there had been in the treaty of 1266, and there seems to have been some uncertainty about ecclesiastical matters. The Scottish crown almost at once after 1468 began to enjoy the temporalities of the bishopric when it was vacant and to exercise patronage; on the other hand, as late as 1662 a conveyance of land in Shetland which had once belonged to the cathedral of Bergen and had fallen to the Norwegian crown was confirmed by King Frederick III.

A key question is whether the sovereignty of the islands was pledged. In 1266 the western isles had been ceded in comprehensive terms, with express exclusion of 'the islands of Orkney and Shetland, which the said king of Norway reserved to his *dominium*, with all their lordships, homages and revenues, services and all their rights and pertinents'.

The marriage treaty of 1281 envisaged the possible cession of 'the whole land of Orkney'. The draft treaty of 1460 proposed to transfer 'all right and *dominium* which the king of Denmark and Norway had in the islands of Orkney and Shetland.' In 1468-9 there is no mention of either *dominium* or 'the whole land'. Christian pledged only 'our lands of the islands of the Orkneys' and 'our lands of the islands of Shetland'. It is even more revealing that the 1468 treaty contains contrasting phrases – 'the islands of the Sudreys and Man' and 'our lands of the Orkney islands'.

It looks as if Norway was ceding something less in Orkney in 1468 than had been ceded in the Sudreys in 1266. It has been argued, not unreasonably, that in 1468-9 all that was ceded was the royal estates, but it is even more reasonable to argue that the 'something less' that was ceded in the northern isles surely embraced sovereignty. Certainly in later attempts to redeem what had been pledged it was more than once claimed that sovereignty had not been renounced and this claim was not, apparently, disputed by the Scots.

Of course in practice Scotland and subsequently the United Kingdom have long and continuously exercised sovereign rights, to the exclusion of any other authority, and it has been said that the union of the islands with Scotland may resemble a marriage by habit and repute but is nonetheless a legal marriage. The documents of 1468-9 are ostensibly 'impignorations' or pledgings, but it has been contended that Christian had no intention of redeeming what he pledged. The treaties certainly omit some of the terminology which would have been expected in a normal 'wadset', as the Scots called such documents: the Orkney document does not even specify the place for repayment, although the Shetland document does.

It is not a novel suggestion that Christian had no intention of redeeming the islands and the question is whether he used an ostensible reversion to cover up his real intention of complete alienation. The earlier negotiations in 1460 had been for a straightforward surrender of all Christian's rights and *dominium* , and it is hard to believe that the Scots government was now prepared to settle for much less.

Christan's position was that he ought not to decide matters touching the Norwegian crown without the consent of his council, nor to alienate or even pledge revenues or fiefs. Whether he obtained Norwegian consent in 1468-9 remains debateable, and it does look as if his device of pledging territory avoided trouble in Norway and saved his pocket to the tune of

50,000 florins by parting with islands in which he had ceased to have much more than nominal interest.

Subsequent events tend to strengthen doubts about the sincerity of the 'impignoration'. Christian had not pledged the lands of the earldom, which were not his to pledge, but in 1470 Earl William St. Clair resigned to the king of Scots his rights in the earldom of Orkney and lordship of Shetland. This meant that if the Danish king had redeemed what he pledged, the earldom would have remained the property of the king of Scots.

Then, in 1472, the Scottish parliament annexed the earldom and lordship to the Scottish crown, specifying that they were not to be given away except to a legitimate son of the king. This of course related to the earl's private property and had no direct bearing on either sovereignty or the international status of the islands. In that same year, 1472, when the archbishopric of St. Andrewswas created, the bishopric of Orkney was transferred to the Scottish province – a strange proceeding had the islands been regarded as genuinely in pledge and liable at any time to revert to Norway.

Yet, whatever the intention of the contracting parties in 1468-9, the process of integrating the islands into the Scottish legal and administrative structure was a long one. It is not until after 1560 that we begin to find a series of acts based on the presumption that Orkney and Shetland were to be treated like any other part of the country. But from much earlier there is evidence that Scottish practice in granting certain privileges and licences to individuals was extended to the islands.

So far as law generally was concerned, it would appear that already in the 1420s – before the impignoration – there was at least a threat of interference with the Norse law which had hitherto operated in Orkney, but the native law seems on the whole to have been retained. In 1468-9 nothing was said either to preserve the Norse law or (as in the Sudreys in 1266) to subject the islands to Scots law.

In 1503 parliamentary proceedings implied that the northern islands were not subject to 'the laws of the realm', and in 1567 parliament evidently had at least some doubts on the subject. There are a number of instances of reference to Norway for legal decisions in particular cases, and the old methods of conveying land were maintained, especially in Shetland, until late in the sixteenth century, though Scottish practice was finding its way in. Both the privy council and the court of session were beginning to give decisions in cases arising in the islands, and Scottish criminal justice was being applied. Not until 1611, however, was the Norse law formally abolished in the islands.

Whatever King Christian's intentions in 1468-9, there had been formally an impignoration, and the Danes frequently attempted to redeem what had been pledged. Danish kings were obliged at their inauguration to attempt to recover the islands, and the Scots never denied that the possibility of redemption existed, but they always tried to shuffle out of their responsibilities and found some pretext for evading the issue.

The question was last seriously discussed in 1667, when Danish representatives, negotiating a treaty with English envoys at Breda, wanted to insert a clause safeguarding the right of redemption. The

English, predictably, protested that they had no instructions in the matter, and the Danes had to be content with a statement that the withdrawal of the proposed clause should not derogate from their claims, which remained whole and entire until a favourable occasion, whether sooner or later, for demanding the restitution of the islands.

XIII LATER ROYAL OCCASIONS

After Norway ceased to have its own royal line, the kind of relationship with Scotland which had existed in the days of Alexander III and Erik could not recur. Yet, in totally different circumstances, Scottish royalty from time to time had links with Norway. The first individual to create such a link was the third husband of Mary, Queen of Scots – James Hepburn, Earl of Bothwell.

One of the many women in his life had been a Norwegian lady. She was Anna, daughter of Christopher Throndsen, a Norwegian nobleman who had distinguished himself in the naval service of the Dano-Norwegian crown, and her mother was the daughter of a dignitary of Trondheim cathedral. Christopher had settled in Copenhagen, and it was there that Bothwell met Anna in 1559 or 1560. Shortly afterwards he had to leave for France to visit Queen Mary, then married to King Francis II.

Anna accompanied him as far as Flanders. Bothwell was later accused of having taken her away from home under promise of marriage, and Anna may well have felt neglected as she languished in Flanders, whence, it is suggested, she wrote a reproachful letter which was subsequently produced as one of the 'Casket Letters' alleged to have been written to Bothwell by Queen Mary.

Possibly in response to such an epistle, Bothwell rejoined Anna, and she crossed to Scotland; then in February 1563 she had a passport for her return to Norway. It may be that she paid another visit to Scotland between 1565 and 1567, but, even when she passed out of Bothwell's life, their liaison was not without its effect on his later career. Lord Darnley, Mary's second husband, was murdered on 10 February 1567 and on 15 May she married Bothwell, universally suspected of being the murderer. Exactly a month later Mary surrendered to rebellious lords at Carberry, and Bothwell fled to the northern isles, of which Mary had made him Duke. He had a narrow escape from capture in Shetland and then made for Bergen.

Unluckily for him, the governor of Bergen was a cousin of the discarded Anna. The outcome was that Bothwell ended his days, a decade later, a prisoner in the castle of Dragsholm at the north end of the Danish island of Zealand; he was buried in the nearby church of Faarevejle, where his alleged remains were on view to visitors (for the equivalent of 6d. a time) until the present Danish Queen ended the disgusting exhibition.

Anna was not the only member of the Throndsen family to have a marital or quasi-marital connection with a Scottish subject. Her sister Else married (apparently as his third wife) Andrew Mowat of Hugoland, who had acquired a large estate in Shetland and who was credited with having had (as his second wife) another Norwegian lady, Karen Gyntelberg.

The son of Andrew and Else inherited property in Norway which was incorporated into a barony of Rosendal, on Hardanger Fjord, but his son by his first, Shetland wife, Ursula Tulloch, inherited his Shetland property. Another sister of Anna, Dorothy, is said to have married a John Stewart in Shetland.

The next episode is again a royal romance. How many people could answer correctly the question, 'Which king of Scots was married at Oslo, in Norway?' The answer is James VI, for whom it had not been easy to find a bride. Any candidate had to be a protestant, she had to bring a good dowry to relieve his financial needs, and she should offer some prospect of armed support for James's claims to the English throne.

While other princesses were considered, one from Denmark seemed most suitable. A Danish match was suggested as early as 1582, when James was sixteen, and in 1585 and 1587 negotiations went on for a marriage to Elizabeth, the elder daughter of Frederick II of Denmark and Norway, whom failing, to her sister Anne.

The Scots asked for a vast dowry, for a guarantee of military aid on a large scale, for the exemption of Scottish ships from the tolls levied on vessels entering the Baltic, and for at least consideration of the status of Orkney and Shetland. No doubt they asked for more than they expected to receive. But in the end they did not do badly, for Anne brought a dowry of £150,000 Scots, which must have represented something like three years' revenues for James, and hard cash was better than promises. The money was, with unusual canniness, lent out to burghs at interest, instead of being squandered.

In 1589, when he was twenty-three, it was arranged

that James should marry the fifteen-year-old Anne.
The marriage was celebrated by proxy in Copenhagen on 20th August 1589, and Anne set out for Scotland, but as time passed and she did not turn up,
anxiety grew. There may have been a fear of a disaster like that in the Patrick Spens ballad.

However, in time word came that Anne's ship had
put into Oslo under stress of weather and that she
was likely to remain there for the winter. James had
by this time convinced himself that he was passion-
ately in love, and lamented his disappointment in
verse: Anne and he were now

> Divided each in divers place.
> The seas are now the bar
> Which make us distance far.
> That we may soon win near
> God grant us grace.

Recalling that his grandfather, James V, had gone to
France to fetch his bride, he made up his mind to
fetch Anne, and, leaving Leith on 22 October, he
landed on 11 November at Tönsberg, where he spent
six nights and attended worship in the church.

On 24 November Anne and he were married in the
old Bishops' Palace at Oslo, a building much altered
and transformed into the equivalent of an English
'Mayor's Parlour'. David Lindsay, minister of Leith,
conducted the ceremony, in French, and the bishop
of Oslo preached. The couple went on overland to
cross the Sound to Kronborg and Copenhagen,
where they spent the winter. John Maitland of Thir-

lestane, James's chancellor, remarked ruefully: 'And here we are farther from home and must have a more longsome, public and perilous voyage in our returning than we might have had out of Norway, which is little above three days' sailing from Scotland'.

James and Anne did not return to Scotland until May 1590. Many Norwegian kings visited Scotland, but James was the only Scottish king (except possibly Robert I) to visit Norway.

It was the last Scandinavian marriage of a British king until Edward VII married the Danish Princess Alexandra in 1863. The consort of the present Queen, Philip, Duke of Edinburgh, is descended in the male line from the Danish royal family, for the first of his kin to reign in Greece was a Danish prince. Queen Elizabeth is the last of the Coburg dynasty (which began with Edward VII), and the next sovereign of Great Britain will, by traditional reckoning, begin a new dynasty of the House of Holstein-Glücksburg.

However, it was neither royal marriages nor royal cruises overseas in the ancient style that led to a resumption of visits to Scotland by Norwegian royalty. The German occupation of Norway in the spring of 1940 (which a British expedition, mounted from Leith, failed to halt) led to the flight of many Norwegians of all ranks by the traditional sea route to the nearest refuge, in Shetland.

Risking the perils of the ocean and the enemy, and often in crazy craft, they crossed in considerable numbers, not infrequently to make a landfall, as adventurers of a thousand years before had done, in Unst or Fetlar. Shetland provided a base, first at

ANNE, Princess of Denmark and Norway, married James VI in Oslo,
1589.

THE CALEDONIAN SOCIETY
OF NORWAY
"GRAND GALA DINNER"

to commemorate the 400th.
anniversary of the
marriage of
King James VI of
Scotland and
Princess Anna
of Denmark
and Norway
at
OSLO LADEGAARD
23rd NOVEMBER 1989

Notice of Dinner to mark the fourth centenary of the marriage of James VI to Anne of Denmark.

Lunna and later at Scalloway, for raids on occupied Norway, and the traffic was such as to merit the name *The Shetland Bus*, the title of a book in which David Howarth related the heroic story. Besides the Norwegians who fled from Norway, there were others who were outside Norway (often at sea) when the German invasion took place, and many of them also found their way to Britain, to form a Norwegian Army-in-exile which had headquarters at Dumfries. In Dumfriesshire as in Shetland there were a good many intermarriages, which have helped to maintain links between the two Countries, and in 1990 Dumfries mounted a Scotland-Norway exhibition.

These wartime associations received royal recognition. Crown Prince Olav of Norway, who had visited Scalloway and given his name to a slipway there, was made a Freeman of Dumfries. He succeeded his father, King Haakon, in 1957, and in 1962, on a state visit to Edinburgh, he received the freedom of the city and an honorary degree from the University. A handsomely produced souvenir of the reception and lunch held in the Assembly Rooms on the occasion included an information note on the historic relations between Scotland and Norway, provided by the Department of Scottish History, University of Edinburgh.

An event of greater historic significance occurred in 1981, when King Olav and Queen Elizabeth met in Shetland. Her Majesty had been duly briefed about the previous visits of Harald the Fairhaired and Magnus the Barelegged, as she called him. The most recent 'royal occasion' was a commemoration in Norway; on 23 November 1989 the Caledonian Society of

Norway (founded in 1946) had King Olav as their guest at a 'Grand Gala Dinner' in Oslo Ladegård, on the site of the old Bishops' Palace, where James VI and Princess Anne of Denmark and Norway had been married four hundred years before.

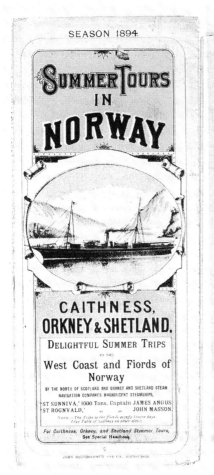

Cruises from Scotland to Norway began in 1886.

XIV COMMERCE AND CULTURE

Wars, treaties, marriages and the movements of royalty, though important, are only a part of Scotland's relations with Norway. However, we can do little more than guess about economic matters in the earlier centuries, though a clause in the treaty of 1266 plainly indicates that shipping between the two countries was of some importance, and the negotiators of the 1312 treaty discussed disputes arising from commercial associations. It is not until the sixteenth century that substantial evidence begins to emerge.

The Scandinavian lands generally and some of the Baltic coasts provided markets for Scottish cloth, skins, grain, coal, salt and fish. In return, from Norway came prodigious quantities of timber.

It was used partly in shipbuilding (although it was by no means unknown for Scots to buy ships which had been built in Norway), but mainly for constructional work in house-building, including the wooden frontages and galleries which were such a notable feature of Scottish burghs in the fifteenth and sixteenth centuries. The timber trade must have been very largely with western Norway and also with Oslofjord; there are references to ports from Trondheim all the way round to Oslo.

The Scottish ports which were involved lay along the length of the east coast. We know, for example, from the Dundee Shipping Lists from 1580-1625 that roughly one cargo in three arriving in the port came from Norway. In the late seventeenth century, for the Firth of Forth ports the Norwegian trade was second only to that with the Low Countries, and for ports north of the Tay Norway had first place.

The reason for the cargoes of timber was not any lack of native timber in Scotland – there was far more of it than is often believed – but it was a question of transport. Apart from what could be floated down from the Highlands by loch and river to places like Inverness and Perth, it was easier to bring timber by sea from Norway than to convey it overland within Scotland. These imports of timber from Norway were vital – so vital that when restrictions were imposed on certain Scottish exports they sometimes did not apply to Norway, so as to preserve a balance of trade with that country.

Surviving Norwegian customs books record the arrival of at least 50 Scottish ships a year, which was a large number in proportion to the total scale of Scottish commerce. And the imports must not be thought of as consisting of undressed tree-trunks. Norway was meeting the needs of its customers by preparing the timber before export, even making use of saws driven by water-power.

So Scotland received 'deals' or boards, 'spars' or planks, 'crukit timmer' or curving branches and joints for roofs and the frames of ships, 'arrow shafts', wooden nails used to fasten slates or tiles, 'pipe staves', which were barrel staves, 'scowis' (probably smaller barrel-staves), 'steyngs' or poles, 'garronis' which may have been poles for scaffolding, and 'wainscot' or good quality boarding (which, however, came predominantly from Danzig rather than from Norway). To judge from what happened elsewhere in areas to which Scots traded, like the Low Countries and the towns on both sides of the entrance to the Baltic, Scots would settle in Norwegian ports, and some appear in the lists of burgesses of Bergen.

While Scottish settlement in Norway was no doubt in the main an offshoot of Scottish trade, and most of the settlers were traders, some Scottish professional men found careers in various places. William Christison, a native of Fife who became minister of Dundee in 1560, had spent some time in Norway, where he found a patron in Geble Petersson, the first protestant bishop of Bergen: he was useful to the kirk session of St. Andrews when it required a translation of a document in Danish.

Some Norwegians of Scottish descent 'surfaced' after their family had been in Norway for generations: the composer Grieg is the best-known example, but Wilhelm Christie, who presided over the Norwegian Storting (parliament) which in 1814 consented to the union with Sweden, was another. Petter Dass, a poet and hymn-writer whose works still have their appeal, was the son of Peter Dundas from Dundee, who arrived in Norway in 1640; he was born in Nord Heröy, an island west of Sandnessjöen, and in 1689 became parish priest in Alstahaug, a few miles south-east of his birthplace.

In architecture, parallels have been detected between the Cathedral at Trondheim and that at Glasgow. Any Scot looking at the Rosenkrantz Tower in Bergen is bound to think that it looks like a Scottish tower, and it may well do so, for when Erik Rosenkrantz was rebuilding it in 1562-3 he engaged masons from Scotland; an armorial panel over the entrance is strikingly similar to panels at St. Mary's College in St. Andrews and the Castle there.

In the same generation Scottish craftsmen were at work in other Norwegian buildings; in 1548 a Scot made a statue of St. John for a rebuilt Franciscan church in Bergen and in 1558 a Scottish mason is named in a list of artisans.

It could hardly be claimed that in respect of migration there was a two-way traffic, but Norwegians have not been insignificant in Scotland. The outstanding name in this connection is Salvesen.

Christian Salvesen, a Norwegian who arrived in Britain in 1851 and took British nationality, began his own shipowning and shipbroking business in Leith in 1872. The name became almost synonymous with whaling, which the firm carried on in various parts of the world for many years and in which field it was a big employer of labour, not least of Shetlanders; for some time now, however, there has been diversification into numerous kinds of business, and enormous vehicles bearing the name Salvesen are constantly to be seen on the motorways today.

Norwegian seafarers frequently came to Scottish ports, and it is significant that the earliest Norwegian Seamen's Church was opened in North Junction Street in Leith in 1886; it continued to serve as something of a focal point for a small Norwegian community in the Edinburgh area until 1985. In recent years large numbers of Norwegians have come to

The Oldest Norwegian Seamen's Church, North Junction Street, Leith.

study at Scottish Universities, especially the Heriot-Watt University in Edinburgh and the University of Stirling, but also Glasgow and Strathclyde.

In a class by itself was the close connection which persisted between Shetland and Norway long after the transaction of 1469. In the late sixteenth and early seventeenth centuries there were families and individuals who had property and interests on both sides of the North Sea and might have been hard put to it to say whether they were Scottish or Norwegian subjects. One example was Christian Johnnson Forsell, burgess of Bergen, who was a native of Yell, where he inherited property from his mother about 1594. There are several references to the 'lordis of Norroway' who owned lands in Shetland and collected rents from them until well into the eighteenth century.

Until the nineteenth century Shetland – where wood was scarce – imported boats from Norway, sometimes in what would now be called 'kit' form, for assembly on arrival, and although Shetland has no shortage of building stone – wooden houses were similarly imported from Norway. One of the channels leading into Bergen is still called Hjeltefjord because it was the route to and from Hjaltland or Shetland.

There were Scottish soldiers in Norway as in most continental countries, arriving as mercenaries hired by the Dano-Norwegian government. In 1568 Axel Wiffirtt, a 'servitor' of the Danish king, was allowed by the Scottish government to enlist 2000 men in Scotland and ship them overseas.

There was competition, for the 'James Ruthven alias Swadin James' of whom we hear in Scotland in 1581 had no doubt earned his nickname by recruiting for the Swedish king. The Thirty Years' War, beginning in 1618, merely heightened the demand and widened the opportunities. First Christian IV of Denmark (brother of James VI's Queen Anne), and then Gustavus Adolphus of Sweden, led the protestant armies, and Scots were recruited into them literally in thousands. But when Denmark and Sweden were at war, as they had been between 1611 and 1613, Scottish soldiers were apt to find themselves on Norwegian soil.

In 1612 some hundreds of Scots mercenaries on their way to join the Swedish service, led by one George Sinclair, were marching through Norway and were cut down by the peasants of Gudbrandsdal. The Norwegian exploit was long remembered in song and story in Gudbrandsdal and Romsdal, and a Gudbrandsdal man later composed a 'ballad', of which certain verses, in translation (put at my disposal by Mr. Knut Campbell) follow:–

> Herr Sinclair sailed over the salt sea:
> His course did stand towards Norway;
> Among Gudbrand's rocks he found his grave –
> A bloody head was inflicted there …

> Herr Sinclair sailed over the blue wave
> To fight for Swedish gold.
> God help you! You certainly must
> Bite the dust before the Norsemen.

> On the coast of Romsdal he made his landfall,

Declaring himself an enemy.
Fourteen hundred men followed him,
All with evil in their souls ...

The farmers came together in Bredebygd
With sharp axes on their shoulders
From Våge, Lesje and Lom;
They wished to have words with the Scot.

The first shot hit Herr Sinclair;
He roared and gave up his soul.
Each Scot cried out when the Colonel fell:
'God save us from this pass!'

Not a living soul came home
To tell his fellow-countrymen
How dangerous it is to visit those
Who dwell in Norway's mountains.

This engagement was commemorated on its 350th anniversary in 1962, when the Edinburgh University O.T.C. traversed the route of the unlucky Scots of 1612.

For a period of four or five hundred years extensive areas of what is now Scotland did not form part of a Scottish kingdom. Orkney was the centre of an earldom which nearly always included Shetland, Caithness and its 'southern land' or Sutherland and sometimes a good deal more. The western isles – 'the Sudreys' or southern isles from the point of view of a power based in the north – constituted a kingdom of The Isles, with its headquarters in Man. Those two Scandinavian dependencies, and especially Scotland's northern isles, lay right at the heart of a North Atlantic commonwealth and were the crossroads of great culture from which they were enriched.

Not only were the islands enriched, but through the islands Scotland as a whole was enriched by the culture of its northern neighbour. Historians have tended to look exclusively to the south for the sources of Scottish culture. It would be no bad thing if they occasionally looked to the north. But even looking to the south they enter a field of Scandinavian influence from settlements in Cumbria and Northumbria. About that influence from the south we know too little, but certain facts should be obvious.

Historians have hardly thought it worthy of comment that the first layman below royal rank known to have built a church within the bounds of modern Scotland bore the unmistakably Scandinavian name of Thor – Thor the Long, who built the church of Ednam, in Berwickshire, in the very early twelfth century. Nor is there any mistaking the Scandinavian influence in the developing Scottish burghs about the same time: the name Swain occurs among the earliest recorded burgesses of Perth, and the term 'kirset', denoting a period during which a newcomer to a burgh could live rent-free while his house was being built, is the Norse *kyrrseta* or *kyrrsaeti*.

The prolonged and close communication of parts of Scotland with the other northern lands had profound, lasting and varied effects. People are so apt to think of the early visitors from Norway as mere marauders, raiders rampaging round our shores, purely destructive and certainly making no contribution to culture. As one immediate corrective to such an idea can be set a memorable fact. Throughout the whole medieval period the Kalendar of Saints was enriched by the names of only four inhabitants of what is now Scotland. One of them was an Englishwoman – Margaret, queen of Malcolm Canmore.

A second was Gilbert, Bishop of Caithness, an area which in his day had only recently ceased to be a part of the earldom of Orkney; his name was Norman and his family seems to have come from Flanders. A third was Magnus, the Scandinavian Earl of Orkney, and the fourth was his nephew Rognvald, who also became Earl of Orkney. Scandinavian Scotland comes well out of the competition for saints, in which native Scots are almost nowhere.

The Scandinavians reached almost every part of

Europe and some lands outside Europe, and were culturally cosmopolitan and eclectic. An eleventh-century earl of Orkney went to Rome and the first native bishop of Orkney, in the next century, was 'a Paris clerk'. A kind of restless mobility persisted after the one-time 'vikings' had become Christians and abandoned their early predatory habits. Their descendants, the Normans, founded kingdoms in Italy and Sicily, went with other west Europeans on the great crusades and established a crusading kingdom in Jerusalem.

One Norwegian king, Sigurd, had a 'crusade' of his own in the early eleventh century and earned the name Jorsalfarer because he visited Jerusalem in the course of a kind of armed pilgrimage which took him, over three or four years, to most parts of the Mediterranean and as far as Constantinople (which the Norse called 'Miklagard', the great city, and where Scandinavians who had made their way overland by the Russian rivers formed a bodyguard for the Emperor). The Orkney earl Rognvald – St. Rognvald, Rognvald the Holy – organised a somewhat similar armed pilgrimage to the Mediterranean in the middle of the twelfth century and – not so very Holy – seems to have had a rollicking good time before he returned to his northern earldom. Thanks to the vivid pages of the Orkneyinga Saga, the genial Rognvald comes to life more realistically than any other twelfth-century inhabitant of what is now Scotland. Thus:

> 'At the gameboard I am skilful
> Knowing in no less than nine arts;
> Runic lore I well remember;
> Books I like; with tools I'm handy;

Expert am I on the snow-shoes,
With the bow, and pull an oar well;
And, besides, I am an adept
At the harp, and making verses.'

One cannot help speculating about chance meetings in the Mediterranean when men faring from various parts of the civilised world would find, in conversation, that they were distant cousins.

Such men kept their eyes open on their travels and wanted to imitate in their homelands what they had seen overseas. With our own eyes we can still see evidence of this in buildings which have survived. If it is true that the first inhabitant of Scotland known to have built a local church was the Scandinavian Thor the Long; it is equally true that the first inhabitant of Scotland known to have built a cathedral was the Scandinavian Thorfinn, Earl of Orkney, who about 1060 erected a 'minster' at Birsay as the seat of the bishop of the islands.

On the Brough of Birsay on the west side of the Mainland of Orkney are the walls of a little church which is something of a gem of romanesque architecture and which cannot be paralleled by anything surviving on the Scottish mainland from that period. There is also in Orkney the remarkable church of Orphir, the only round church of medieval date in Scotland. There are round churches in other lands, including England and Denmark, but the concept seems to have jumped completely over mainland Scotland to crop up again in Orkney. Modelled on the church of the Holy Sepulchre in Jerusalem, it is not fanciful to see the Orphir building as the consequence of a Mediterranean excursion.

Round Church at Orphir, Orkney: east end.

But the best corrective for anyone who thinks of
Scandinavian influence as destructive of culture is to
look at the cathedral in Kirkwall, built (or at any rate
begun) by the crusading Earl Rognvald, in honour of
his uncle, St. Magnus. The general character of the
architecture, in the 'Norman' fashion of the period,
indicates that the building would not have been out
of place anywhere in western Europe, for it was the
product of a cosmopolitan civilisation. Yet, whatever
inspiration derived from what far-travelled men had
admired in distant lands, it was simpler to bring
architects and masons from areas easier of access,
and experts agree that the chief elements in the first
phase of building at Kirkwall derived from Durham,
in part mediated through Dunfermline or other buildings in what we now call Scotland.

The term 'north Britain' is more appropriate for a
period when the Anglo-Scottish frontier – if there was
one – was not the present Border and when Scotland,
subjected first to Anglo-Saxon, then Anglo-Scandinavian, and finally Norman influence from the south,
had peculiarly close links with Durham.

The splendour of Kirkwall's cathedral, and its testi-
mony to the wealth and prosperity of Orkney and the
culture of Orkney's rulers, are brought out if compa-
risons are made. It was conspicuously superior to any
of the other more remote or peripheral Scottish cath-
edrals. It must be contrasted for example with Lis-
more, where the cathedral was a gaunt two-chamber
building, consisting of only a choir and a nave and an
insignificant western tower – no aisles, no transepts
and only 130 feet long (compared to Kirkwall's 218).
That was the best the diocese of Argyll could do.

'Cubbie Roo's Castle' (12th century), Wyre, Orkney.

It is perhaps hardly fair to compare Kirkwall with Iona (115 feet), for the church there was not designed as a cathedral and became one only late in the day and by accident. It is a meagre and in some ways not very tasteful building, deficient in decoration as well as size in comparison with Kirkwall. The same can be said of Dornoch (126 feet) and of Fortrose (120), though in the first case heavy restoration has effaced its original character and in the second the remains are too fragmentary to allow a clear impression of the whole building. One can also make a comparison with that other cathedral dedicated to St.Magnus, at Kirkjebour in the Faroes, which can be described as a somewhat ornate box with windows in it, modest in size and without much distinction, but even so the Faroese never managed to finish it.

There was also important secular building in

twelfth-century Orkney. It has been claimed that the earliest square stone castle in all Scotland is on the island of Wyre – 'Cubbie Roo's Castle', authenticated from the Saga as having been built about 1150 by one Kolbein Hruga (and with a soundly constructed church nearby). Comparing it with the wooden towers of the mottes of contemporary Scotland anyone who wanted to score a point could say that while noblemen in Scotland were still living in wooden shacks, this gentleman in Orkney built for himself a miniature stone keep. If we knew more about the other early stone castles of which meagre remains survive in the north and west our impression of comparative standards of architecture might be extended. Perhaps the strongest competitor for the title of the earliest stone castle in mainland Scotland is Castle Sween, in Knapdale, but that may also be of Norse origin, the work of a northerner called Sven and not of an Irishman called Sweeney.

While there is no reason to doubt that expert workmen were sometimes imported, it is more than likely that they would find apt apprentices among the natives, for there is ample evidence of the skill of Scandinavians in various crafts, not least carving. Anyone looking at some of the artefacts found in ship-burials and at the workmanship in some of the Norwegian stave-churches sees examples of the seemingly interminable interlacing and the weird and fantastic zoomorphic patterns which are found also on some Pictish stones, in the Sutton Hoo burial in East Anglia, in Irish artefacts, in the illumination of volumes like the Lindisfarne Gospels and on 'Celtic crosses'. No race seems to have had a monopoly of such designs.

Traces abound today of the extensive Norse settlements within what is now Scotland, and traces too of
the ancient North Atlantic culture of which these
settlements formed a part.

The original Scandinavian speech, once universal
in the three northern Scottish counties, died out
between the fifteenth and the eighteenth centuries,
and the spoken tongue there is now basically a form
of Lowland Scots – often a somewhat archaic Lowland Scots dating from the period when that tongue
was introduced and with occasional features which
suggest that the imported tongue was sometimes
imperfectly understood – but especially in Shetland
there is a strong admixture of Norse words and
idioms. When a Shetlander says 'enoo' he is not
giving a rendering of the English 'even now'; he is
using the 'endnu' still current on the other side of the
North Sea. And when he uses 'follow' meaning to
accompany, as in the phrase, 'I'll follow you home',
or when he says 'Lock the door' meaning merely
'Close the door' and not 'Turn the key' he is using
Scandinavian idioms and not being illiterate in English. On his lips and on those of Norwegians, 'gate'
means a road and the equivalent of the English 'gate'
is 'grinnd'.

The most immediately obvious evidence is that of
place-names, which recur in country after country.
Fuglöy in Norway and Faroe, Foula in Shetland; each
with the same name, meaning the bird island, and
presenting a great cliff to the western ocean. Perhaps
the most impressive group is composed of Tingwall
in Shetland and in Orkney, Dingwall in Easter Ross,
Tynwald in the Isle of Man and Thingvellir in Iceland,
each commemorating a meeting place of early 'things'

or assemblies. Then we have Collafirth in Shetland, Kjöllefjord in the far north of Norway, Kollafjördur in Faroe; and so on almost *ad infinitum*. There are, besides, plenty of generic elements familiar by frequent repetition: 'wick' meaning an open bay, 'fjord' or 'firth' meaning a longer and narrower inlet, and the suffixes ' -ness' meaning a peninsula and ' -a' or '-ay' meaning an island. One moves around over vast stretches of land and water and all the time feels somehow at home.

Investigation is required as to whether the constant repetition of names always arises simply because identical physical phenomena were labelled by early settlers with identical descriptive names, or whether some of the repetition arose because migrants took names with them and gave them to places near their new homes. Possibly scholars who are prepared to use their eyes as well as their ears might be able to determine whether names which are ostensibly descriptive are really descriptive or were transferred by the migrants from other places in the north. It has been pointed out that some place-names in Faroe seem to represent conscious imitation of the pattern of place-names in Shetland. The same may perhaps have happened elsewhere and if so it may throw light on the pattern of migration.

Yet with all the repetition of standard elements in place-names, there are differences too. Orkney and Shetland each have groups of names which are far more common in one archipelago than the other, 'quoys' in Orkney and 'voes' in Shetland for example – and Caithness too had its peculiarities. On the whole Shetland seems to conform more to the pattern prevailing in other lands, while Orkney and Caithness are more eccentric.

Does this again throw light on migration? In that connection, perhaps variations in place-names might be paralleled by physical characteristics. Of course the notion that all the people in all the northern lands are tall, fair-haired and blue-eyed is nonsense. It certainly seems that there is a dark strain in all those lands, including Norway, Faroe and Iceland, and one is apt to find in any of them people who closely resemble the dark people one sees in Shetland. Certainly the idea that every dark Shetlander or Orcadian is descended from a shipwrecked sailor of the Spanish Armada cannot be entertained for a moment. One wonders whether some of the dark strains noticeable in the west highlands and islands may also have an affinity with the dark people of the northern lands.

The intensity of Norse survivals of every kind varies a good deal from one area to another. In Orkney and Shetland and most of Caithness the Norse penetration must have been so complete as almost to obliterate the earlier inhabitants, and the place-names there are almost 100% Norse. In Sutherland the mountains and the lunar landscape of the west did not appeal much to discerning migrants, who probably never went far inland, and consequently the impact was limited. South from Sutherland on the east coast there was some Norse settlement on both sides of the Moray Firth, but beyond that perhaps, apart from the somewhat startling 'Kyrkenes' in the heart of Fife – it is difficult to find traces until we come to the Lothians and Berwickshire, where there

St.Magnus Cathedral at Kirkjubour in the Faroes.

were offshoots of the Scandinavian settlements in the north of England.

In the west the pattern was different. In the islands a large proportion of place-names are Norse – in Lewis some 80%, Skye about 66% and Islay about 33%. Some have been modified by Irish influence: the suffix ' -ness' is found in Skipness, Kintyre, but elsewhere it is modified into ' -nish' as in Trotternish and Waternish; 'wick' produced Brodick, but in Skye it is modified into Uig. On the mainland off which the islands lie, names of Scandinavian origin are rare, even in semi-insular Kintyre, but there are some ending in '-nish' (Craignish) and many ending in '-dale', which may not have had a directly Scandinavian origin.

There are plenty of Norse elements in the south-west mainland, such as '-bec', meaning a stream (Allerbeck, Merebeck), ' -by', meaning a settlement (Sorbie, Canonbie), ' -thwait', meaning a clearing or a meadow, which becomes 'that' and 'what' (Howthat, Butterwhat), and '-fjell', a hill, which becomes the familiar 'fell'. The many parish names in the area which have 'Kirk-' as their first element, often followed by a saint's name, are also claimed as representing Scandinavian influence. In the south-east a number of personal names may have represented secondary migration from the north of England rather than settlement direct from Scandinavia.

The west has preserved Norse personal names as well as place-names. The progenitor of many MacLeods had a Norse name, Liot (borne also by an abbot of Brechin). Other west highland names of Norse origin are Ronald (Rognvald), MacManus, son of Magnus, and MacAulay, son of Olaf (a name pronounced Ola or Ollie in Orkney and Shetland). Torquil is the Scandinavian Thorkild, and MacCorquodale is Thorkettill's son. Lamont is good Scandinavian for 'the lawman' an important piece of history effaced by those who ignorantly or obstinately accent the name on its second syllable. All the evidence suggests that in the west Norse penetration was less effective than it was in the north. Probably there was a more numerous native population there when the Norse arrived, and the incomers were very likely fewer.

The impression one forms is that outside certain areas the immigrants formed a kind of ruling aristocracy, not numerous but influential. The natives survived and mingled with the immigrants to form a mixed race, and the native tongue, derived from Ireland, survived, though it took in some Norse words and gave some words to Norse. It was a mixed race, under the leadership of magnates of partly Norse blood, who formed the people of the western highlands and islands when they first began to appear identifiably in history in the twelfth and thirteenth centuries.

Evidence from personal names is naturally more plentiful in the northern isles than in the west. Christian names, chosen by parents and passed on through the generations, are apt to be peculiarly tenacious, despite social and linguistic changes, and Shetland long preserved names unfamiliar or even unknown in Scotland: Magnus, most popular of all northern names, remains common today, and going back a couple of centuries or so one finds Erasmus, Erik, Erling, Ola, Paul, Sewald, Sheward, Swen and

Theodore among men and Brita, Ingagar and Sunniva among women. Surnames long continued to
preserve the Scandinavian tradition not by their presence but by their absence, for in Shetland as elsewhere in the north most people were designated by
patronymics formed from the father's Christian name
plus ' -son' or ' -daughter', as is still the practice in
Iceland.

Patronymics were common in Shetland in the seventeenth century and did not die out until the nineteenth. The writer's great-great-grandfather, William
Donaldson or Danielson, who was born in 1770, was
the son of Daniel Theodoreson.

Apart from speech and names, survivals from Scandinavian times are to be found in various artefacts. A
flail from Norway and one from Shetland are hard to
differentiate, and it has been noted that the same
type of flail was used in Ireland, Orkney, Lewis and
Norway while a different type was used in
Perthshire, Glenlivet, Cumberland and Durham. Perhaps it is less convincing that a sickle hardly changes
its shape throughout the northern regions, but the
similarity in the primitive oil lamps in Norway, Shetland and the western isles is striking. Even more
impressive is comparison of plunger churns from
Norway, Shetland and Iceland. An ouskerry, an
implement for bailing a boat, had to be fashioned to
fit into the narrow bottom of the boats constructed on
the traditional northern model, and specimens constructed in earlier days of wood in Shetland are precisely paralleled by plastic examples now on sale in a
ship chandler's in Bergen (and sometimes used as
scoops for fish in fish-shops).

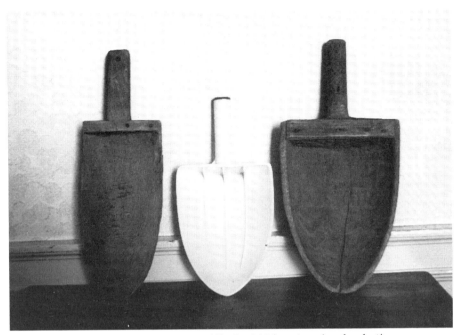

Two wooden bailers or 'ouskerries' (Shetland 19th century.) and a plastic specimen (Norway, c. 1970).

Of course it is the boats themselves which remain the most conspicuous sign of the old connections, and this is appropriate, since the whole culture was based on movement by sea. Very much the same type of boat can still be seen in all the northern countries. Modifications, devised to suit local conditions, make it easy to distinguish Norwegian, Shetland, Faroese and Icelandic boats, and even within each country there were minor local differences, but the common ancestry, in the vessels which carried the early migrants a thousand years ago, is unmistakable.

Survivors are now dwindling, to be replaced by moulded hulls, designed for the motive power of engines and not for either sail or oars. Specimens of native design are becoming rarer in Norway and even in Shetland, while in Greenland, where the boats

Boats on a beach in Iceland.

must at one time have been of Scandinavian type, it is now difficult to find such a craft. The great stronghold of tradition, in this as in other matters, seems to be Faroe, where the people not only preserve boats with ten or twelve oars in museums but use them on the water and where the standard powered boat, with an inboard engine, still retains the old design.

In the western isles, the Norse longships, clinker built of wood, were taken over in place of boats constructed (as in Ireland) of skin. They may have undergone some modification, for as shown on the graveslabs they have more perpendicular stems than their ancestors, but that may be the result of compression by the sculptor.

In the west, naval rather than military service regularly featured in charters, which sometimes prescribed the provision of a galley with so many oars. An act of parliament of James I, in 1429, ordained that all barons and lords with lands in the west and north should have galleys,

'that is to say of ilk four merkis worth of lande ane aire [oar], ande that is til understande of thaim that are nocht [in]feft of galeis before, for thai that ar infeft of before shall kep and uphalde the galayis that thai are infeft of and haldyn to sustene be thair auld infeftment. And that the said galayis be maid and reparalyt be Maii cum xii moneth ... And the landis and lordshippis whatever thai be strekande endlang the cost syde and inwart in the landis six myle sal contribute to the reparacion ande sustentation of the said galayis'.

This was eloquent of a sea-based society and means of warfare. Boats of the Scandinavian type

survived in the western isles until fairly recently:
some vessels used there as ferry boats in the nineteenth century look remarkably like Shetland sixareens.

In Scotland as in many other countries the character
of life in the present has been largely shaped by
migrants who in past centuries introduced their own
languages and cultures. Nothing at all is identifiably
indigenous. In the gloom of the first centuries of the
Christian era we can discern, in the land south of the
Forth and Clyde, Britons whose language was the
ancestor of Welsh; most of the land lying north of the
Forth was occupied by Caledonians or Picts, of whose
material culture there are ample remains but whose
original language has left hardly a trace except in
place-names, though many Picts acquired the Welsh
of their southern neighbours the Britons.

Both of these races were incomers; the Britons are
believed to have come from the south and the Picts to
have reached Scotland by a northerly sea route from a
homeland in eastern Europe – 'South from Scythia' as
Bede put it. In or about the sixth century A.D. more
identifiable migrants arrived: Irish, called 'Scots',
came across the North Channel to settle in the west of
the country, bringing their own tongue, and English
or Angles came over the North Sea bringing their
Germanic language to the south-east.

Both of those languages had a great future; Irish
spread into the centre, the north and the east and
even made a brief and limited incursion into the
south-east; the tongue of the Angles, from which
stemmed both English and Lowland Scots, spread
rapidly up the east coast ond ultimately came into use

Boats on a beach in Shetland.

over all Scotland. Migrants from Scandinavia followed not long after the Scots and the Angles, and their influence has been the subject of this book. The next to come were those second-hand Scandinavians, the Normans, whose language and culture have been characterised as generally French but might better be styled 'Gallic'. With them came a contingent from Flanders.

There were no more significant immigrations until the nineteenth century, which brought hordes of Irish and some Italians, Poles and Lithuanians, and in the twentieth there came more Poles and, later, many settlers from furth of Europe.

Migrants were not the whole story, for there was influence from France and the Netherlands through commercial and cultural links, but, while the languages of those countries did give some words to Scots, the French and the Netherlanders (except some Flemings) were hardly significant numerically as colonists. The major influences were those of peoples who colonised in some numbers – Irish, English and Norwegians. The Norwegian language, though for centuries the main tongue in many areas, proved to be less tenacious than the first and second and was relatively easy to assimilate to speech derived from the tongue of the Angles, which it resembled.

Domination belongs now to the languages which developed from the speech brought in by the Angles and which are understood by all save a tiny fraction of the population. For many generations prophets have been proclaiming the imminent demise of the Scots tongue, but it has proved remarkably tenacious, and in recent years, despite considerable social and official discouragement and without any artificial stimulus whatever, it has shown many signs of revival in speech and even in writing. It hardly makes sense to speak of any other tongue as a runner-up to English and Scots, for their old rival, the tongue introduced by Irish immigrants, is now in effect on a costly life-support machine and no more than about 1½% of the population claim to understand it. The day may not be distant when a stronger challenger than it will emerge in some language introduced by Asian immigrants.

BIBLIOGRAPHY

Most of the source material for the earlier period, including copious extracts from the Sagas, was conveniently brought together by Alan Orr Anderson in *Early Sources of Scottish History A.D. 500 to 1286* (2 vols., Oliver & Boyd, 1922). There are convenient editions of Snorre Sturlason's Sagas *The Norse King Sagas* and *The Olaf Sagas* in the Everyman Library. Of *The Orkneyinga Saga* there are several editions: that by Joseph Anderson (Edinburgh, 1873) had the most appropriate literary flavour, but Alexander Burt Taylor's (Oliver & Boyd, 1938) is more critical in both text and notes and the modern reader is well served by the edition produced in 1981 by H. Palsson and P. Edwards.

T.M.Y. Mason, *Drifting alone to Norway* (Lerwick 1986), tells the adventures of Betty Mouat and earlier 'castaways', including St.Sunniva.

The general story of Norwegian expansion is recounted in Johannes Brondsted, *The Vikings* (Pelican), in Gwyn Jones, *The Norse Atlantic Saga* (OUP, 1964) and, with unforgettable illustrations, in *The Viking,* compiled by a team of experts and published by Wahlström and Widstrand, Stockholm, 1967. The incursions into the British Isles by 'Vikings' and 'Danes', who were often in truth Norwegians, figure largely in the standard histories of England by Frank Stenton *Anglo-Saxon England* and of Scotland by A.A.M. Duncan *Scotland: The Making of the Kingdom* and A.P. Smyth *Warlords and Holy Men* (Edinburgh Unversity Press). There is a scholarly survey of Scandinavian Scotland by Barbara E Crawford (Leicester University Press) and the volume she edited on *St.Magnus Cathedral and Orkney's Twelfth-Century Renaissance* (Aberdeen University Press, 1988) includes an article on 'The contemporary Scottish scene'.

There is a very comprehensive guide to all the material on The Maid of Norway in Sir Archibald Dunbar, *Scottish Kings* (1899, 1906; pp103-9). The Treaty of Perth of 1266 is printed in translation in Dickinson, Donaldson and Milne, *Source Book of Scottish History* (vol I; pp 34-6, 117-8) and in Donaldson's *Scottish Historical Documents*, (pp 34); William Fraser's letter of 1290 appears in translation in those same works (vol I, pp 125-7, 41-3). There is a facsimile edition of the *Chronicle of Melrose*, edited by A.O. and M.O. Anderson (London 1936).

The complete Latin text, with a translation, of the treaty of 1468, pledging Orkney, is in John Mooney, *Charters and other Records of the City and Royal Burgh of Kirkwall* (Kirkwall, 1950). The historical context and the sequel to both that treaty and the pledging of Shetland in 1469 are examined by G. Donaldson,

'Problems of Sovereignty and Law in Orkney and Shetland' in *Stair Society Miscellany Two* (1984).

Useful information about commerce between Scotland and Norway is available in S.G.E. Lythe, *The Economy of Scotland 1550-1625* (Oliver & Boyd, 1960); and T.C. Smout's *Scottish Trade on the Eve of Union* (Oliver & Boyd, 1963).

Guidance in the vast field of place-name studies is given by W.F.H. Nicolaisen, *Scottish Place-Names* (Batsford, 1976).